Principles of Spiritual Leadership

Assuming Your Spiritual Responsibilities

A Guide for Spiritual Growth & Development

B.Y. Stuart, PhD LCPC
Inspirational Series for Personal Development

We are all called to serve, no matter what title we hold. Let us work diligently to please God & bring glory to Him
By Barbara 2012

Principles of Spiritual Leadership

Assuming Your Responsibilities

A Guide for Spiritual Growth & Development

****

Faith Restoration Ministries [FRM] Inc
Copyright © 2009 B.Y. Stuart, PhD LCPC
Ordained Minister
Conflict Management Consultant
Counselor
Author
Radio Host

Other Publications by this Author

Grace: God's Unmerited Favour
The Power of Prayer
Fruit of the Spirit
Workplace Abuse
Managing Difficult People
What is Love?
Spiritual Warfare
Cry the Beloved wife: Domestic Abuse in the Pew
Betrayal of Sacred Trust
The Chosen Vessel
TEN Questions to ask myself before I say I DO
Fruitfulness
When the Circle Breaks

Principles of Spiritual Leadership

Assuming Your Responsibilities

A Guide for Spiritual Growth & Development

Copyright © 2009 B.Y. Stuart, PhD LCPC
Faith Restoration Ministries [FRM] Inc

Printed in the United States of America

ISBN 1449591078

What does God Require?

What doth the Lord require of thee, but to fear the Lord thy God, to walk in all his ways, and to love him, and to serve the Lord with all thy heart and with all thy soul...(Deuteronomy 10:12, 13).

I therefore, the prisoner of the Lord, beseech you that ye walk worthy of the vocation wherewith ye are called, (Ephesians 4:1).
Thou therefore endure hardness as a good soldier of Jesus Christ (II Timothy 2:3).

Table of Contents

Steadfastness

"But thanks be to God, which giveth us the victory through our Lord Jesus Christ. Therefore, beloved brethren, be ye steadfast, unmoveable, always abounding in the work of the Lord, forasmuch as ye know that your labour is not in vain in the Lord"
[I Corinthians 15:57-58].

Excellency of Spirit

"Then this Daniel was preferred above the presidents and princes, because an excellent spirit was in him; and the king thought to set him over the whole realm"

[Daniel 6:3].

Faithfulness

"Now when Daniel knew that the writing was signed, he went into his house; and his windows being open in his chamber toward Jerusalem, he kneeled upon his knees three times a day, and prayed, and gave thanks before his God, as he did aforetime" [Daniel 6:10].

A Special Note

Outside of God, no one person knows everything. There are still many uncharted waters, mountains to soar, depths to fathom, valleys to span, rivers to wade, and terrains to discover which you do not know.

Therefore, God raise up His people who will impart His knowledge and wisdom to help build His Kingdom.

Principles of Spiritual Leadership is an inspirational text God has given to us to help in the leadership and guidance of His people.

Principles of Spiritual Leadership gives information on leadership directly from biblical concepts with examples from those whom God has used in the past for His glory.

Every leader who is serious about spiritual leadership will find that *Principles of Spiritual Leadership* contains a volume of knowledge and wisdom for the leader God has called to guide, direct, and instruct His people in preparation for the coming of Jesus Christ.

Those who are seeking to be successful and to please God will discover that *Principles of Spiritual Leadership* brings a different approach to spiritual leadership.

Principles of Spiritual Leadership was inspired by God and directed by the Holy Spirit.

To God be all the Glory, Praise, and Honour

Barbara Stuart
2009

Part I

Preparing to Lead

Objectives

The Word of God teaches us to study to show ourselves competent to do the work of the Lord. Moreover, the word tells us that the people of God perish due to lack of knowledge. Therefore, the aim of Principles of Spiritual Leadership is to help leaders assume their God-given responsibility to lead, teach, correct, and direct the people in their charge. With the help of the Holy Spirit, we can do all things because we know that greater is He who is in us, than He that is in the world. The objectives for this manual include the following:

1. To define and describe the awesome role of Spiritual Leadership
2. To prepare leaders for their calling
3. To explain leadership dynamics
4. To identify ministries in the church
5. To teach Conflict Management Skills for effective leadership
6. Examples of Leadership
7. To describe the Nine Gifts of the Holy Spirit in Leadership
8. To reveal leadership pitfalls
9. Self Assessment Profile

Responding to Your Call

One of the most significant indications of an effective spiritual leader[1] is that he/she must be a visionary, with the ability to delegate and motivate for positive interpersonal relationships and harmony in the Body of Christ. Jesus was the perfect model for leadership.

"Leadership in the body of Christ is a high calling, which requires a high level of commitment. We cannot serve the devil six days a week and serve God on Sunday.

If we want our lives to be useful and productive in the Lord's service, we cannot chase after the amusements and fashions of the world. It will not work to pursue our own pleasures and ambitions first, and seek the kingdom of God as a second priority.

We must also keep our *bodies* unpolluted by defiling habits, our *minds* unsullied by defiling thoughts, and our *hearts* untainted by defiling affections that would make us unsuitable for use in the service of God.

Righteousness, faith, love, and peace are the qualities God looks for in His servants.

Finally, the basic qualification for service is consecration. Have you consecrated yourself to the service of God? There must be a voluntary act of submission to the will of God and a devotion to His service above all other interests or pursuits."

"I urge you, brothers, in view of God's mercy, to offer your bodies as living sacrifices, holy and pleasing to God – this is your spiritual act of worship" [Romans 12:1, NIV].[Cited from Adult Student Sunday School, December 2005-February 2006, COGOP]"

---

[1]Leader here is considered as *anyone* called by God, Holy Spirit anointed and controlled, with Christ-like attitudes, and who has a specific duty in the Body of Christ in the local church for the spreading of the Gospel.

1

Leadership Dynamics

Leadership with a Christ-like Perspective
Preparing to Lead

Leadership dynamics give an outline of the Christ-like qualities a true Spiritual leader should possess. This is by no means complete and there are many other characteristics that could be added to this list for the spiritual leader. Every leader should bear in mind that to be effective and to please God he must be called, prepared, anointed, and appointed by Him for his leadership office.

L – Learner - *to be wise*
(Proverbs 1:5). It is important that the leader is disciplined with a willingness to be a learner before he/she decides to take up a position in leadership. To be an effective learner there must be readiness to listen in order to discover knowledge, and to gain understanding with wisdom for application.

E – Example – *to be a pattern of good works*
Every leader must be willing to set applicable examples for others to follow. He or she must be diligent about setting the right behaviours which others can emulate. It is vital to make every effort to develop self-control and good character – (Titus 2:7, I Timothy 4:12-16). He should display examples of good conduct, order, modeling effective behaviours, self-discipline, attitude, warmth, sincerity, and loyalty. The leader will be even-tempered, obedient, respectful, devoted to the calling, courteous, and an observer of confidentiality. These qualities will attract others to him.

A – Attentive – *a listener*
The leader must be a good listener to the Holy Spirit. There must also be sensitivity when giving instructions to others. He must pay special attention to the words used to communicate and the way in which he speaks to those

he is leading (Proverbs 15:1, James 1:19). The attentive leader is alert, watchful, dutiful, caring, observant to the needs of others, empathetic, and alert to the feelings of others.

D – Discerner – *test the spirits*

The discerning leader does not accept everyone to place in positions since so many false prophets and deceivers who claim to be Christians are a reproach to the Name of Jesus Christ. The Holy Spirit will reveal falsehood if he is listening and obedient (Matthew 24:5, I John 4:1).

E – Excellent Spirit – *approachable*

The spiritual leader must demonstrate self-control and compassion. He must not be easily led or act with impulsivity or be judgmental (Daniel 5:12, 6:3). The leader will not allow anger to control his behaviour. Instead he or she will seek to prevent or appease strife (Proverbs 15:18, 17:27, 28).

R – Reliable - *dependable*

The leader must be constant, stable, committed, punctual, considerate, and conscientious (I Corinthians 15:58). These include being dependable, faithful, consistent, loyal, trustworthy, and steadfast.

S – Servant-hood – *willing to serve*

Spiritual leadership is servant-hood which means the person must do everything in his or her power to be like Jesus Christ and serve His people. He must be a person of integrity who can be trusted (Job 27:5-6). Therefore, his word must be truthful with genuineness and earnestness without incongruence or ambiguity. He must be a teacher, qualified, capable, skilled, prudent, discreet, informed, and impartial.

H – Humble – *non-competitive*

Since this person has to interact with people of varying personalities, cultural, economical, and educational backgrounds, communication skills, and styles of communication, he must be humble. There must also be frankness and a determination to fulfill plans, willingness to help, friendliness with warmth and sensitivity, kind, loving, generous, courteous, patient, without partiality or hypocrisy (I Peter 5:6). The humble leader is one who is approachable and agreeable with meekness and gentleness. This person must live a life of faith (Hebrews 11:1, Mark 11:22-24). Always bear in mind that humility is strength and not weakness.

I – Intercessor - *prayerful*

The leader must be an intercessor not only for the self, but also for the people he leads. Examples of intercessor include (Daniel 9; Jeremiah 14:7-9, 19-22; Moses - Exodus 32:30-33; Jesus at Lazarus's grave John 11; over Jerusalem Luke 13:34; for Himself; His disciples; and all believers John 17).

P – Perceptive - *observant*

The perceptive leader is sensitive to the needs of others and insightful. The leader must be a visionary with godly wisdom (James 3:17). He must be prayerful and should encourage his people to exercise faith by his own example. The perceptive leader is insightful with a keen awareness of what is happening under his leadership.

Review

1. Describe the insights you gained from these dynamics.
2. What other spiritual qualities do you think are missing from list?
3. Explain your understanding of servant-hood.
4. What is the difference between servant-hood and being sub-servient?
5. Explain why God expects His leaders to be servants.
6. Do you see yourself as a servant of God or as a CEO?
7. Where you see your leadership from the information given in this list?

2

Definition of Christian Leadership

Firstly, to define Christian leadership, we must look at this quality from the biblical perspective for the manner in which God's servant <u>administers</u> *doctrinal*, *spiritual*, *godly* and *moral* principles to His people.

The person who desires to lead, or who is called to lead God's people must know that spiritual leadership is completely different from secular.

Outside of spiritual leadership, the world's expectation is for profits in the corporations. In sports, the coach must excel with winnings; otherwise he is out of a job if there are too many losses.

In comparison to spiritual leadership, the leader's ultimate accountability is to God. Therefore, it must be described as a gift from God through the Holy Spirit just as all other spiritual gifts (I Corinthians 12:4, 11).

Moreover, the uniqueness of Christian leadership requires love, wisdom, strength, endurance, patience. The leader must be humble (Romans 12:3), and one who does not respond to world's standards (Romans 12:1-2).

Spiritual leadership can be a lonesome experience with lack of thankfulness from those who are selfish and insensitive. For this reason, he must be willing to face trials, tests, hardships (II Timothy 2:3), and such like all for the sake of pleasing God and being obedient to His will. These are some of the qualities which make this type of leadership unique.

Secondly, spiritual leaders create the *mission* of the ministry and outline the *strategies* for its attainment through the power, wisdom and guidance of the Holy Spirit in the Name of Jesus.

Thirdly, Christian leadership is one of <u>servant-hood</u> for the Lord: *"For we preach not ourselves, but Christ Jesus the Lord; and ourselves your servants for Jesus' sake"* [II Corinthians 4:5].

Therefore, the leader proclaims through his behaviours, the qualities pertaining to what Jesus would demonstrate especially that of humility (John 13:4-8).

Fourthly, the main goal for Christian leadership is the <u>winning</u> of souls and <u>preparing</u> God's people for the return of Our Lord and Saviour Jesus Christ.

Finally, the mission of the church incorporates the <u>holistic needs of its people</u> such as spiritual, emotional, and other situations that will develop in its midst.

3

Spiritual Gifts

"Now there are diversities of gifts, but the same
Spirit. And there are differences of administrations,
but the same Lord. And there are diversities of
operations, but it is the same God which works all
in all" [I Corinthians 12:4-5].

The church is the earthly representative Body of Jesus Christ. Being an organism, it is alive and actively engaged in the winning of souls. Everyone may not be visibly working, but the work is going on all the time.

Peter described Jesus Christ as a "living stone" (I Peter 2:4-5). Within this living Body, God has equipped the church with many gifts with each one being a ministry working with others *"for the perfecting of the saints, for the work of the ministry, for the edifying of the body of Christ"* (Ephesians 4:12). Spiritual gifts are from the Holy Spirit for the effective working of the church.

Function of the Church
The function of the church is complex because while it is the spiritual presence of the Body of Jesus Christ, all its work is not spiritual. It must function in a world of sin where there are myriads of situations in the community that will require the help and service of the members. The church must also be considered a hospital for sick souls with diverse and varying degrees of conditions.

One of the major things that leaders must bear in mind is that the church, God's people, belongs to Him. Therefore, the leader must focus on God for direction, guidance, and empowerment through the Holy Spirit. He should give place to the manifestation and operation of the gifts in the church (I Corinthians 12:8-10), and not stifle those whom the Holy Spirit will use.

Too many church leaders are only concerned about pleasing "certain" members in order to keep them; instead of adhering to the will and pleasure of God. Those leaders will hold services around the desires of their "special" people, and totally ignore the will of the Holy Spirit. Is it any wonder that many churches are "dead" even with thousands of members?

Purpose for the Gifts

Spiritual gifts are not to be held privately as *earned* prized certificates for personal endeavours. The gifts are for edification, nurturing, training, administration, and the development of godly leaders for the service of the Lord as is mentioned in Ephesians 4:12. In order to strengthen the church those gifts should be working actively under the inspiration of the Holy Spirit.

Description of the Gifts

The gifts are diverse in their *administration*, *operation* and *manifestation*; but they *all* work in harmony with and empowered by the Holy Spirit, and not exclusively. Also, each gift has a specific function, but works in unity for the growth, nurture, development and maturity of believers (I Corinthians 12:4-6).

Stay in Your Gift

Each member should know his or her specific gift and work in that position (Romans 12:6-8). We operate in a gift according to the grace given to us by the Holy Spirit through faith.

Empowered by the Holy Spirit

Moreover, no gift can be effective without the empowerment of the Holy Spirit (I Corinthians 12:4, 11). He is the one who selects, decides, and administers each gift proportionately to everyone. Nevertheless, in order to be effective, the leader must walk in the Spirit (Galatians 5:16) and not in carnality.

God's Desire

With so many gifts within the Body, I believe that God's desire is for them to be used to the fullest and for His glory. It is obvious that one person, e.g. a leader cannot and should not attempt to do *all* the work in the church by himself. The leader's job is not to be burned out for God, but to be used by God for His glory and His praise.

Setbacks, Trials, and Tests

Although the church has been given many spiritual gifts, effective leadership comes with setbacks, defeats, trials, tests and multicoloured experiences (II

Timothy 2). There are also trial and error situations due to differences in human traits and personalities relating both to the leader and those whom he leads.

Occasionally, we will find leaders who were not called, ordained, appointed or anointed to lead God's people. Situations such as those will certainly cause problems especially if the leader is arrogant, and does not have administrative interpersonal skills to lead others.

Obviously, he would not be under the leading and guidance of the Holy Spirit. Nevertheless, the leader who has been called by God, and has an open mind for learning [teachable spirit] will use each experience as a lesson to gain insightful information that will be helpful to the ministry.

Spiritual leadership is challenging and requires courage, patience, love and the Holy Spirit. This type of leadership involves commitment, reliability and consistency. It is important for any church to have proper spiritual leadership. However, selection must be made from among those who are capable, willing, mature and godly; and who are ready to use their gifts for the effective administration of the work in the Body (*See Acts 6*).

Review
1. Do you allow the manifestation of spiritual gifts in the church?
2. What guidelines do you give to your people for the operation of spiritual gifts in the church?
3. Do you have the spirit of discernment to identify gifts in the church?
4. Do you know your specific gift/s, and operate in them?
5. When selecting individuals for positions in the church, what specific qualifications do you seek for?
6. How can you tell if an individual has the gift he or she professes to have?
7. Do you believe education should precede spirituality when choosing an individual for a position in the church?
8. Discuss the purpose for spiritual gifts in the administration of the church.
9. In what ways do spiritual gifts help your work as a leader?

Figure 1
Ephesians 4:11
And he gave some, apostles; and some, prophets; and some, evangelists; and some, pastors and teachers.

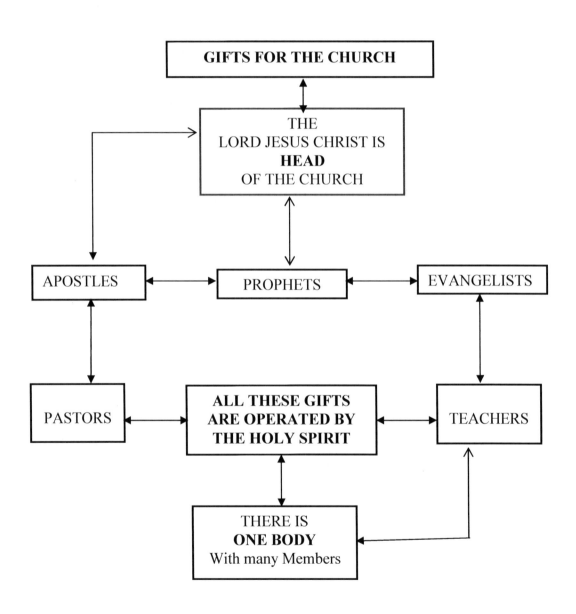

GIFTS FOR THE CHURCH

THE
LORD JESUS CHRIST IS
HEAD
OF THE CHURCH

APOSTLES

PROPHETS

EVANGELISTS

PASTORS

**ALL THESE GIFTS
ARE OPERATED BY
THE HOLY SPIRIT**

TEACHERS

THERE IS
ONE BODY
With many Members

4

Structure of Spiritual Leadership

"Let no man despise thy youth; but be thou an
example of the believers in word, in conversation, in
charity, in spirit, in faith, in purity"
(I Timothy 4:12).

The Holy Spirit

According to Galatians 5:16, Paul instructs us to *"Walk in the Spirit, and ye shall not fulfill the lust of the flesh."* Therefore, the leader must seek to please God before the self with a willingness to do His will. *[Be thou an example of the believers],*[2] are strong words. This means to be a *pattern*, a *blueprint*, a *template* of true effective spiritual leadership. The possession of a title only identifies in the natural sphere, but spiritually it has no power. The leader's power lies in his obedience to the Lord and being controlled by the Holy Spirit.

Although the Holy Spirit gives gifts to the church, there must be order and structure in the form of demonstration concerning the operation and administration of each gift. I Timothy 4:12, identifies six essentials for the effective demonstration of Spiritual Leadership namely: *word, conversation, charity, spirit, faith, and purity*, including other graces which will be discussed below. These guidelines do not refer only to titled leaders, but to everyone who has been called into ministry such as ushers, choir members, Sunday School teachers, and so on.

Paul was very careful to include the types of behaviour that was expected of the leader after encouraging Timothy not to be deterred by anyone who would ignore his calling. He told him "let no man ***despise*** thy youth" or let no one undermine your ability in God.

To despise means to loathe someone or in this case your gift. It means to look down at you scornfully with hatred. It means that your leadership capabilities may be held in derision because of the contempt others have for your ability or your

---

[2] I Timothy 4:12

methods of administration. In effect, Paul is saying do not allow peoples' behaviour to hold you back from your calling, and the work God gave you to do.

If you will be a successful spiritual leader, then you must be an example to other believers. This is exactly what Paul is saying to every leader; thus revealing the importance of effective modeling in the structure of your performance. The admonition is for all leaders to be examples not only to believers, but also to the world (Colossians 4:5). Furthermore, Jesus said: *"Ye are the light of the world..."* (Matthew 5:14a). Wherever and whenever we interact with people, we are always on display whether in the home, at church, work or in the public's eye.

Knowledge of the Word

We cannot be effective leaders if we do not *study* the word, *understand* the word, *know* the word, *believe* the word, *meditate* upon the word, and *apply* the word to our lives. Every leader must take time to read and study God's word in preparation for service and on a daily basis. Nonetheless, he must not find himself trapped in useless discourse of the Word or be easily led by false doctrines, or demonic teachings which only bring destruction and spiritual death.

It is important to note that merely reading the word is not sufficient. Instead, the leader must be knowledgeable with the understanding on how to apply and impart God's Word to others. This is done through the experience of learning (II Timothy 2:15). Time must be taken to study and memorize for effective application (Colossians 4:6) with the use of various tools such as commentaries, concordances, and dictionaries to help with the explanation and meaning of words.

Prayer

Prayer must be an essential part in the life of the leader to keep in communication with the Lord (Luke 18:1). It is vital because it is the spiritual life-blood that brings oxygen to give him spiritual strength to overcome temptations and remain strong against trials. There must be special effort made to pray and seek God's will in all his ministerial administration (I John 5:14-15). He must pray for himself, the church, the community, governments, other leaders and the Body of Jesus Christ. The leader must *always* pray for souls to come to Christ.

Fasting

The act of fasting may not sound very popular in this day of gluttonous behaviour. Nevertheless, fasting is a spiritual discipline which was practiced since the earliest of times by the prophets (Joel 2:15, Isaiah 58). Jesus Himself encouraged fasting (Matthew 6, Mark 2). Paul in his résumé, indicated that he fasted often (II Corinthians 11:27), meaning it was part of his spiritual life.

Fasting is a discipline which requires humility and commitment. It is an expression of submission to God in seeking His will for making decisions, getting closer to Him, and building strength for the tasks as they come.

Fasting is also soul-searching and seeking for higher levels with the Lord. It will strengthen and motivate the entire Body of Christ to give the best service. Leaders should encourage fasting in the church.

Self-Discipline

The conduct of the leader must be exemplary in every detail of his life so that the name of Jesus is not reproached. *Holiness* is a requirement for the life of the leader and this means that he is not conformed to world's standards. Instead, he lives in obedience, and faithful service to Jesus Christ. A life of holiness requires discipline because the leader knows that he or she should not behave as the world. To be called to spiritual leadership is a holy calling and this work must be carried out with discipline, courage, and diligence. There must be attentiveness to duty and carelessness must be to the minimal. Therefore, the leader should seek to maintain a holy life at all times for active relationship with the Lord (*See* Galatians 5:22-23).

Confidence

The leader without confidence will lead others astray. If he is unsure of his performance he should seek the Lord for wisdom and courage. He must know that God is his help and if he trusts His guidance, he will not be afraid to confront, persuade, correct, rebuke, and reprove (II Timothy 4:2). These are administrative duties he must perform to change the minds of difficult members with the use of effective arguments to motivate and stimulate them to live for the Lord (II Corinthians 5:11).

Moreover, the leader who is confident will be *gentle* towards others. He will be diligent and faithful to his commitment, and will not take advantage of the weak.

Gentleness will make him into a great person because he is not easily moved or broken by insults nor will he use harsh words to others. His gentleness will help to instruct those who are contrary and who cause strife in the church (II Timothy 2:24-26). Furthermore gentle words wield great power.

The confident leader is not motivated by flattery; but he places complete reliance on God. He is *even-tempered* and does not engage in outbursts of anger nor does he seeks to retaliate. He recognizes that vengeance belongs to God, and trusts Him to vindicate his cause.

Confidence makes the leader behave *respectful* and he conducts himself with decency making others respect him. He has an agreeable temper with courteous behaviour even in those times when he is being insulted by others. He must not deliberately hurt others in word or deed, nor should he give occasion for offence (Philippians 2:15). The confident leader depends on the Holy Spirit for direction.

Wisdom

The leader who uses discretion in all matters is a wise person (cf. Nehemiah 2:12-16). There are times when he has to be alone to examine, plan, and make decisions before incorporating others. His aim is to seek God's wisdom before proceeding on certain tasks as Nehemiah did. This action will avert many sorrows and disappointments. A wise leader will control his emotions, and this effort will keep him from being easily overcome by anger (Ephesians 4:26-27, 31). Also, he will teach with boldness without fear of reprisals or shame (II Timothy 1:8). When he knows that he is working under the influence of the Holy Spirit there will be courage and willingness to confront and silence with all authority, those who cause discord and confusion; yet in the spirit of love (Ephesians 4:15).

Active Faith

We read in Hebrews 11:1 that, *"Faith is the substance of things hope for, the evidence of things not seen."* Additionally, *"Without faith it is impossible to please God…"* (Hebrews 11:6). Faith demonstrates commitment to God, and confidence in His promises. It represents loyalty and belief in His word. If we have faith, then we must demonstrate it in our behaviour, speech, and conduct with others. It is *faith* that will make us believe the *word*, to apply it in our conversation in *love* and with the right *spirit*. Every leader must live a life of faith in order to be an effective example.

Purity

Purity means morality, chastity, and upright behaviour especially when interacting with the opposite sex. This refers to cleanliness, wholeness, and truthfulness. In I John 1:16 we read of the three things that will destroy a leader *"...the lust of the flesh, and the lust of the eyes, and the pride of life."*

The observation of purity will help the leader flee fornication and all manner of sexual sins. It is also important to keep the thoughts clean by controlling imaginations, so that wrong thoughts do not dominate your life (Philippians 4:8). Purity will guide the leader away from filthy lucre and the "get rich quick" mentality seen on so many programs. It will deliver him from greed and ill-gotten gain.

Charity

When we hear of the term "charity" we quickly think of giving to those who are unfortunate with less or none of the world's bounty. Indeed it does mean giving. Charity is offering kindness to others, even to the one who hurts us.

The leader who does not take time to offer sympathy, compassion, understanding, tolerance and so on to others, is not Christ-like. That person is an impostor to spiritual leadership.

Some of the so-called spiritual leaders of today only put on the collar and the title of Reverend; but lack the mere essence of Christianity or charity. For many, the members cannot call on them when they are in trouble.

There are also those who will call up members for tithes if they have been missing, but do not ask about their welfare or why they were absent from church. This is not charity.

If a leader treats his own members in this fashion and then go to some foreign country to give "charity" that person's religion is a farce. That person is a hypocrite.

If you say that you love everyone, and you truly mean this, then respond to the questions below and see how you rate.

1. How do you demonstrate care and compassion to your members who pay tithes in the church?
2. How many of your members do you know, and in what capacity?
3. How often do you meet with your members, and can they call upon you in a time of trouble?
4. In this time of economic poverty for the majority, in what ways are you expressing "charity" to those in your church, and leaders of smaller churches?
5. Can you accept God's unconditional love to give it to others?
6. What does John 3:16 means to you?
7. Do you recognize the elements of forgiveness, patience, generosity, and kindness in John 3:16?
8. How would you show the love of God to others who are of a different
   a. religion,
   b. skin colour,
   c. culture,
   d. language,
   e. geographic, educational, economic and social background?
9. Do you hold resentment, and grudges against those who have offended you?
10. Do you overcome evil with good or seek opportunities for revenge?

Review

1. List the skills needed for effective leadership. Can you add more?
2. In what ways do Christian leaders differ from secular? What are some similarities?
3. Can secular administrative skills be used in spiritual leadership?
4. Explain in what ways secular skills would be effective and when they would not work?
5. Can you truly say that you are an effective role model to other leaders?
6. What is the structure of leadership in your church?
7. Is the Holy Spirit in control of your life?

Check your Leadership Performance

1. How has the word changed your lifestyle – thought, behaviour, emotions, concern for people, your family and your ministry?
2. How do you interact with others – business, work, church, and home?
3. Do you give as you receive – tit-for-tat?
4. Do you obey what the word says to you?
5. Can people take you at your word – to trust, and depend on what you say?
6. How do you as a leader speak to others?
7. Do you create confusion, strife, and chaos because "you are only human?"
8. Are you arrogant, impatient, unkind, harsh, and angry with those who do not understand you?
9. Do you use cutting, insulting words, which devour your hearers?
10. Do people have to use a shield to approach you?
11. Do you hit first and ask questions after?
12. Are you judgmental so that you speak before hearing?
13. What is your conduct in a conversation?
14. Do you cut into a conversation untimely?
15. Do you make sure that you express yourself before others?
16. Do you always want to win an argument?
17. Can you control your emotions?
18. Are you argumentative, or do you try to understand others?
19. Do you allow God to handle a situation that might get out of hand?
20. Are you willing to say, "I am sorry?"
21. Are you truthful with your feelings?
22. Do you allow personality to dictate to you, either yours or others?

5

Spiritual Characteristics

Although leaders are expected to be self-motivated as well as being a motivator, it is important for them to behave Christ-like in their interpersonal relationships and business transaction. He must be a visionary with clear insights to where he wants to go, how he will get there, and the resources he needs to accomplish his goals. Still, he must always bear in mind that he is the servant of God; therefore he must be willing to serve the people. He must also be willing to ask for help and deal with criticisms.

Christ-likeness

True Christian leadership reflects and portrays a servant with a heart and characteristics of Jesus Christ incorporating attitudes of compassion, kindness, empathy, and faithfulness. The true servant never forgets that Jesus Christ is his leader; and that to be great in His employ means being a servant (Matthew. 10:42-45). The leader is committed to His work by being kind, understanding and caring for those whom God has put in his care whether it is a large or small group.

The main factor for Christ-likeness is faithfulness to this commitment (Matthew 24:45-47). Good servants are loyal to their masters and therefore, the servant of God must be loyal to Him. Furthermore, as the representative of God, it is imperative that His people are treated with respect and not with duress or intimidation; especially since the leader is accountable to God for his service (Acts 20:28). Take the following into consideration for Christ-likeness:

1. Serving others (Matthew 8:1-15)
2. Training others (Matthew 10:5-42)
3. Humility (John13:1-16)
4. Not greedy of gain (I Timothy 3:3)
5. Mentoring (II Timothy 2:2)

6. Jesus was a model Servant-Leader (John 13:2-17)

7. Affirming others into leadership roles (Matthew 10:1-42)
8. Obedience (John 14:15)

Preparedness

For everything we plan to do, preparation is necessary. Spiritual preparation is vital because people are often demanding and intractable. The Bible teaches how Jesus prepared Himself soon after baptism before calling the disciples (Mark 1:19-13). He spent time in fasting and prayer, and if He needed to prepare then His leaders ought to do the same. Furthermore, there are situations that will try the moral, spiritual, and emotional fibre of the leader, and he will need to be strong to face those situations when they appear.

Interpersonal Skills

The leader must have effective interpersonal skills that will attract others to him. For example, when Jesus chose His disciples, He did not compel them. On the contrary, He simply said, *"Follow Me, and I will make you fishers of men"* (Matthew 4:19).

Interaction with Members

In addition, the leader must not be distant from the members. He should not be passive and allow problems to go unresolved while people are being hurt. Preferably, he should be involved with the spiritual development of the members with teachings to reach each one at all levels. He must show sincerity and honesty, with an intense interest to help, a passion to love and maintain harmony, and unity to build positive relationships. These cannot be achieved in isolation. He should make attempts to know his members and set up times when he makes himself available to them.

Problem Solver

The leader must be a problem solver even if he does not have answers he should be able to help with advice and or referral. Working with people can be a hard task and leading them presents an even greater challenge because people are different and some are very difficult. The leader must be able to transform people and events by engaging and drawing them into specific roles. The leader must be able to *influence* rather than coerce; *lead* rather than compel; and be *informed* rather than assume. Also, he must be an encourager while being open to encouragement, wisdom, and counsel from others.

Spiritual Standards

The spiritual leader must not be attracted to worldly philosophies, which are *conceived* in pride, *birth* in arrogance, and *applied* in ignorance. This type of leadership does not meet the standards of God. He should not conform to principles that only weaken the spirituality of the members.

For example, there are leaders who introduce worldly music and ideas dressed in Christian garb, and branded as "ministry;" but they are really worldly concoctions. They do this to "please" the people because they want to have members in the church.

Seemingly, the Holy Spirit is no longer capable to bring convictions to the hearts of sinners; therefore those leaders are replacing the Spirit of God with their own wisdom. Clearly, the spiritual leader must be transformed [Romans 12:1-2] in order to follow spiritual standards by taking the following into consideration.

1. First, the Holy Spirit must be the source of power to guide and direct him as he seeks the will of God in decision-making (Proverbs 3:5-6); instead of relying on worldly standards or innate knowledge.

2. Second, he must consider his position as one of servant-hood (Luke 22:24-27) as opposed to world-view standards.

3. Third, he must submit to Jesus Christ (James 4:7).

4. Fourth, in contrast to the world, the Spiritual leader must use the Scriptures as his chart (See II Timothy 2:15).

Dealing with Difficult People[3]

One of the ways in which the leader will be severely tried is with people who are difficult to get along with anyone. Admittedly, everyone is different and each person desires to be served. However, as a leader he must know his limitations and understand that there are times when he has to say 'no' gracefully. I Corinthians 13, Galatians 5:22-23 are passages to study and embrace. The leader must understand that the structure of his leadership is God first, family next, and ministry last.

---

[3] "Managing Difficult People." Available @ www.themarriagecorner.web.officelive.com

Other Leadership Qualities

1. *Be an effective example* (Titus 2:7). No one will follow a leader who does not exhibit Christian behaviours before his members. When there are internal, personal, or family problems the leader should make every effort to be discreet in terms of how he resolves those situations. Some things which are delicate should be kept within the boundaries of the community, home, or self.

2. *Teacher* (Titus 2; II Timothy 2). Every leader should be willing to transform lives through teaching of the word. The effective teacher will change the lives of those who hear him Nevertheless, if he is to be a good teacher the leader must show willingness to learn,.

3. Be a *servant leader* – in the New Testament we learn that Jesus is the greatest model of a true servant leader.

4. *Do not harm* others (II Corinthians 6:3-10). Be sincere in all you do.

5. *Peaceful* Do everything in your power to live in peace with everyone (Romans 12:18).

6. *Delegate* (Luke 9:1-6). It is very important to acknowledge gifts in the church so that the leader can train and delegate (Titus 2).

7. Be *faithful* Despite the hardness of your experience; stay focused and faithful to the Lord. The leader must endeavour to serve God with sincerity and loyalty.

Review

1. On a scale of 1-10 with 1 being the least, how would you rate your leadership skills?
2. What can others say about your performance as a leader?
3. Do you believe you should be a servant? Explain your response.
4. Do you delegate work for others to do, or you do everything for yourself?
5. Do you believe that your ministry should come before your family? Why or why not?

6

Facing Change

While Joshua was Moses' minister for many years; the time came when he took up the mantle to either continue with the strategies used by Moses or to be innovative and trust God to direct him.

Undoubtedly, there will be some hesitation, however minute when someone takes over leadership from a predecessor who had successes or even failures. The hesitation maybe due to fear of the unknown; and even wondering where to begin in the new position. Nevertheless, the leader who is called by God need not fear because He would never leave his side.

Resistance

Change is not always welcome by people who are constantly complaining. Whatever methods that were used and worked before may not work for you. You must be prepared for oppositions and defiance from those who are not willing to move forward, but who will do everything to keep the status quo. If you have to make changes after a leader has left for whatever reasons, you must be strong and not fearful of anyone who might intimidate or cause problems.

If God has called you to the position then you must depend on Him to guide, instruct, and lead you (Psalm 32:8). Never try to fill someone else's style to be like, act like, to sing like, and so on. Seek to please God first and give yourself to prayer. God will teach you and reveal to you how to fulfill your calling into the position.

Change can be Challenging

If previous methods have become institutionalized, you may find that you cannot make necessary changes because of oppositions. Unless the people were having a difficult time with the previous leader, your greatest hurdle may not be the river Jordan or the Red Sea, but people who refuse to adjust or to see things your way. What will you do then?

I believe this would be the time to seek God's wisdom and favour so that decisions will not bring division. Spend time to build trust and confidence with the new members. Even if you were part of the membership before, they are expecting you to work miracles, to make things better, or they will stand in the way of your progress. You must be courageous and put your trust implicitly in God and follow His direction. Do not allow people to cause you to lose your anointing or weaken your walk with God.

Change means that you are leaving the known into the unknown, the familiar to the unfamiliar. There is always some measure of fear, anxiety, and stress. There will be resistance from members to accept the new, after being comfortable with what used to be. Do not yield to those who are instruments of satanic schemes. People may even conspire against you, but do not fear. Trust in the Lord.

Review

1. If you are starting in a new position or taking over from someone, how optimistic are you that you will be successful?
2. On what principles do you base your plans for leadership?
3. Are you willing to accept advice from people who might not be as educated as you, but who have proven to be godly and spiritual?
4. How would you face the oppositions that may come to this change in your life?
5. What preparations did you make before stepping into this are of work?
6. If you had been in leadership before, what were your successes and failures? How did you handle both?
7. What did you learn from your last position?
8. Will you use the same strategies in this new position even if they will not work with the people you will be leading?
9. How will you motivate the people to trust your leadership? Will you ask for help?
10. Do you possess the qualities required for this particular position?
11. Are you a learner or over confident that you know everything about leadership and does not need to learn anything new?

7

Some Pitfalls in Leadership

Some leaders go out of their way to meet the needs of every one at the expense of their own health, family, and ministry. They do not spend time in prayer and seeking God for His leading and direction.

Every member is not conscientious in caring for the welfare of the pastor. There are those who believe the pastor is responsible for all their welfare and even their family. They want him to be everything, even their chauffer. No one can meet the needs of everyone. Only God who can and there are times when, because of the hardness of peoples' heart, He cannot satisfy them at all. How then can anyone even attempt to please everyone?

Over-Busy Syndrome

Leaders are often so busy they do not have time for themselves or their family. Many years ago I listened to a missionary who spoke with regret that he had not had time for his family. The leader should never get so busy that he does not have time for God or his family. You cannot please all the people all the time. You will only please some of the people some of the time. Do not be over-committed.

Poor Family Life

Some leaders spend more time in and with the ministry than with their family. This is wrong! Being a Christian does not mean there should not be time for rest; and recreation especially with the family.

Poor Health

Many leaders seem to think that their bodies were made out of steel, so they do not take care of themselves. Even steel gets a bit tarnished at times. Leaders must rest at some time. There was a time when Jesus saw how hard the disciples were working and He told them *"Come ye yourselves apart into a desert place, and rest a while..."* (Mark 6:31b).

Lack of Time Management

Control your time and set priorities. Leaders should arrange time efficiently in order to avoid stress and depression. Often when people are depressed it is anger turned on the inside because they are constantly living on their nerves. After a while the body rebels against the constant barrage of emotional and physical pain. Time management is vital for the leader. This means that in order to achieve goals and complete plans, he must set priorities, delegate to others, and observe the meaning of time. Start on time, and complete on time.

Poor Approach

The leader who has a poor approach is unfriendly, aggressive, and distant with a cold and insensitive attitude. That person is often consumed with himself, and hardly has time for others. This is wrong if the leader intends to be a success or to please God. This style of leadership is often controversial because of ambiguity in communication and intent. To avoid these situations he must be specific about his leadership style and what he requires of those who work under his administration.

Lack of Delegating

One of the most significant indications of an effective spiritual leader is the ability to delegate; Jesus was the ideal model for delegating. This skill will motivate others for positive interpersonal relationships and harmony in the Body of Christ. Every organization requires the highest level of motivating and transforming leadership for a group to survive and thrive. In the church this trait is often lacking and pastors are burned out at times before reaching their highest potential.

Review

1. What changes do you need to make to avoid the pitfalls leaders often made?
2. What will you need to do to spend more time with
   a. God,
   b. your family, and
   c. your ministry?
3. How is your health?
4. Do you train others so that you can delegate when needed?
5. Why do you train others?
6. When you seek to please difficult people what effect does this have on your
   a. spirit,
   b. emotions,
   c. family, and
   d. ministry?

8

Preparing to Lead

"For which of you, intending to build a tower, sit not down first, and counts the cost, whether he have [sufficient] to finish [it]?" (Luke 14:28).

No one in his right mind would take on a leadership position without first knowing the objectives and goals of his mission in order to decide how he will accomplish his program. He must also decide what kinds of resources he will need such as people - knowledge, skills, experience and attitudes; time; finance; space; equipment; and material. Moreover, his plans must be made clear to those who are involved.

Next, the leader must be prepared to persevere and face the storms of being a leader especially when suffering comes. Obviously there will be many times of tests and trials that will bring feelings of abandonment, loneliness, and even discouragement (Note II Corinthians 4:8-10). In his preparation, the leader should take the following into consideration:

Setting Goals and Objectives

Every leader must have a goal or objective in mind that will guide him in his preparation. If there are no goals set, then he is working haphazardly with no concern for success or failure. The teacher who prepares students has a goal that one day they will succeed and graduate. Similarly, God desires His people to be wiser than the world. He tells us in His word that "*If any of you lack wisdom, let him ask of God, that gives to all men liberally, and upbraideth not; and it shall be given him* " James 1:5. The setting of goals gives a picture of where you are going and what you need to get there. Think about the following:

1. Ensure you *know* where you are going and *how* you will get there.
2. Decide how will you begin to achieve those goals?
3. What do you need in terms of
    a. Equipment;

b. Human; and

c. Financial resources?

Staffing: Acts 6:1-8

The leader should seek God's guidance to direct him in the selection and appointing of his staff.

He must

1. Prepare a description for each position and the qualifications required.
2. Be obedient to the leading of the Holy Spirit (Psalm 32:8).
3. Decide if training is necessary and what type.
4. Decide who to delegate to help him realize the vision?

Choosing other Leaders: Acts 6:3

Be prayerful when selecting individuals who may only have the right intellectual qualifications and motivational interests, but lack the spiritual aspects for your plan. Despite the educational abilities, if that person does not have the Holy Spirit as guide, you might suffer losses which may take you a long time to recover.

Training

The leader must be prepared to select and train individuals for positions in the ministry. He should not force his will on anyone, but rather allow the Holy Spirit to work in the heart of individuals. Training should be set up to meet the needs of the ministry.

The Purpose for Planning

1. There are many instances when God made plans even though He *knows* the future and is not limited by time or circumstances. He instructs in the building of the Ark, the Tabernacle and other situations. If God made plans, then as mortals the leader should follow His example.
2. Since time moves so swiftly, it is vital that it is used wisely. Planning is therefore important when it comes to the timing of events, and how those will be taken care of.
3. Since no one person can effectively operate a church, the leader must plan to teach and train others to follow him. Additionally, he should hold meetings with other leaders to discuss progress, setbacks, and future plans.

Effective planning requires collaboration with others, sound counsel (Proverbs 15:22, 24:6); and effective listening (James 1:19).

4. The leader must take into account that the best prepared plan can fail because although the leader has the right resources and people, people are subject to weaknesses. Therefore, planning and prayer must be intimately related. Prayer leads us to seek God's wisdom and direction.

5. The leader must have faith when he makes plans; otherwise, it is futile making plans if he does not believe he will accomplish his objectives (Hebrews 11:1).

6. Although planning is for a future event, this should not prevent the leader from being hopeful and trusting in God who does not fail. God will be with him as He was with all other leaders before him, for example Joshua.

7. Planning is necessary because it helps the leader to make checks to see what has been accomplished against the goals and objectives for his programs.

Control

The act of panning is essential, but there must also be control because this action will serve to influence the performance of the group. The leader needs some mechanism for checks and control to ensure that each person knows what is required, understands the program, and is going into the same direction.

The leader must demonstrate by his interest in each member of staff that he knows what is happening, and understand the morale of the group. He needs to find out if there is cohesiveness, discontentment, or any viewpoint that will impede the work and affect interpersonal relationships. Furthermore, to wander aimlessly without planning, checks, and control is asking for problems and chaotic situations to develop. A measure of control helps to recognize problems that may develop in the process either with the plans or with the resources.

Responsibility

Leaders are responsible to see that those in their charge are properly guided in their spiritual growth and development. Responsibility also means overseeing those who are in charge of various activities pertaining to the growth and development of the group. Very often members are placed into positions which they are not interested or in any way qualified. Those persons will operate for a while, but later give up for some ridiculous reasons. It is therefore, the duty of the leader to identify incompetence, lack of spirituality, low morale, and indolence. These will be evidenced from performance reviews and control.

Mentoring

The leader *must* ensure that there are mature godly members who display skills and values to share, and who can help with the mentoring program (*See Titus 2*). However, he may sometimes have to counsel to help solve problems and to encourage.

Members Responsibilities

The leader should see that every member shoulders his or her own responsibility to walk faithfully before God. No leader should compel members, nor should he have to feed them with milk throughout their lives.

Confidentiality

One of the major qualities of an effective leader is confidentiality. He must be able to keep important information and not spread gossips and rumours that usually cause injury to others and reproach to the Name of Jesus whom He represents.

Evaluating

This process is another form of control because it measures the performance of each member of the staff. The results help to set clear guidelines for any necessary changes into the structure of the plan; and to remedy any problem situations that pertain to the completion of a program. It will show whether the job is being done properly; if individuals are getting along and cooperating with the program; if team-spirit is strong; whether participation of each member is equal, and if they are efficiently handling problems that may have developed.

Accountability

The Bible teaches that Christian leaders should be accountable both to God and also to God's people whom the leader serves. Among the requirements Paul describes for a Christian leader are that he be "blameless," and "of good character" (I Timothy 3:2). It is important to bear in mind that the Christian leader must *"have a good testimony among those who are outside, lest he fall into reproach and the snare [net, lure, trap] of the devil"* (I Timothy 3:7). The leader is accountable for personal sins, and should make every effort to live a clean life before the members and those who are without. It is important that he demonstrates integrity and honesty and must prove himself worthy of the name of Jesus whom he represents.

Personal Accountability

1. *Spiritual Life:* The leader must set apart time each day for prayer to read and meditate. If the leader is deficient in these areas he will be barren and unfruitful (II Peter 1:9). It is the relationship the leader has with the Lord that will make him a fruitful branch (*See* John 15).

2. *Work life*: If the leader works in secular or a church setting, he has the responsibility to live a life reflecting Christ-likeness. This is not meant only in his speech, but also in his conduct, conversations, habits and attitudes. Does he have the mark or essence of being a Christian on the job? What are colleagues saying when he is absent?

3. *Disciplinarian*: Discipline is not meant to be negative. Rather, it shows special care for those who have done wrong or who seem to be going in the wrong direction. The exercise of discipline serves two purposes both for the church and for the person who has been corrected. First, discipline helps the leader to keep order; and second, it helps the one who has been disciplined to see himself and make right with God. Nevertheless, if the leader fails to practice church discipline this will be disobedience of God's will.

Rules

1. Explain the rules governing the behaviour of members and ensure that these are understood by everyone.
2. Be willing to teach and support new members.
3. Explain requirements for membership.

Communication

1. Effective interpersonal communication is vital for the smooth functioning of and the accomplishment of your vision.
2. Always communicate changes and requirements in a timely fashion to leaders/members.
3. Do not assume each person understands or knows about the activities and rules of the church.
4. Use bulletin boards, emails, announcements, and telephone calls when necessary.
5. Avoid the temptation of working independently of your administrative group or [board].
6. Do not take anyone for granted, but treat each one the same way you would like to be treated. This means with importance.
7. Listen, listen, listen and listen.
8. Be congruent when communicating. Body language is a great indicator of intentions.

Members' Needs

1. Everyone has basic needs such as companionship, fresh air, water, food, sleep, but do not try to fulfill all the needs of the members. Allow them to help themselves.
2. Find out why a member or some members are irritable. Ask what you can do to alleviate tension or even person needs.
3. Motivate members to be involved and excited about your vision.

Making Decisions

This is a very critical time for any leader and for the program. Therefore, decisions must be made with the full assurance that you have the support and interests of the people you are leading.

1. Be open to constructive criticisms. Listen attentively to concerns and avoid being arrogant since you do not know everything. Even God is patient and longsuffering to everyone. This is one way in which you can reach mutual agreement and create harmony among members and you.

2. Seek to win your peoples' trust rather than their mere approval especially if this is given under duress or fear.

3. Get to know your members, and try in every way to work with and not against them. Otherwise you will have the position as leader, but lack support, respect, and interest of the people for you and your program.

4. Always involve the most important persons in your planning and then move on to the larger group. Nevertheless, always involve everyone when necessary so that no one is left in the dark about the program.

5. Be careful how you present any new plans or projects at any time.

6. Look for those who are experienced and excited about your project, with a willingness to participate by using their knowledge and skill.

7. Be a person of integrity, and work with people with similar qualities.

8. Test the spirits [I John 4:1]:
    a. Does your staff adhere to the same doctrinal beliefs as you do?
    b. In what ways do you differ?
    c. What is the Holy Spirit revealing to you?

Review
1. How will you inform and motivate others of your vision?
2. Do you have interpersonal and administrative skills for others to work with you?
3. How do you plan to treat your staff to maintain morale?
4. Do you include all the staff in your decision-making process or only those who are directly related to the plans?
5. How do you select your staff?
6. How do you communicate your plans to members of your staff?
7. What is your relationship with members of your group?

9

Selecting Workers

Jesus did not leave His Disciples in confusion concerning the ministry and what He required from each of them. In John 6, He revealed His plan by first encouraging them that "...*He that believeth on me hath everlasting life*" (v. 47).

Following that information He said "*I am the bread of life...the living bread which came down from heaven...Verily, verily, I say unto you, 'Except ye eat the flesh of the Son of man, and drink His blood, ye have no life in you'*" (vv. 48-53). The passage reported that "*From that [time] many of His disciples went back, and walked no more with Him*" (v. 66).

Information is vital for effective team building. Let the people know from the beginning what you require of them. Give them the opportunity to decide if they want to be with you or not. Do not deceive, but be honest and sincere concerning what you require of each one to achieve your goal. You must be a person of high integrity.

Moreover, no leader will be effective if there is no clear information concerning his intentions for the group and their obligations. The leader must remember that each person who obtains membership in a group has needs, and expects those needs to be met during the life of the membership.

Take the following into consideration when making selections:
Thoughtfulness
Every leader who cares for his followers will be considerate and thoughtful about their welfare. Jesus saw how tired and spent His disciples were and said **unto** them "*Come ye yourselves apart into a desert place, and rest a while*" (Mark 6:31).

In another situation, Jesus had compassion on the people who listened to Him all day on the mountain side. He made sure they did not go away hungry [Matthew 15:32] to prevent them from fainting on the way.

Appreciation

The effective leader will recognize those who are working earnestly to meet the goals for his vision. This will motivate and encourage his staff to work earnestly.

Discerning

The Spirit of discernment will be an asset to the leader because it will show him those persons who will build or sabotage the work. The leader who lacks this gift will meet with many troubling situations, and may even lose the very vision he was trying to bring forth. According to I John 4:1 *"Believe not every spirit, but try the spirits whether they are of God...."* There are members who profess to have been saved for many years, but their lives do not represent spiritual growth and development. Seemingly, they are still being fed with milk. The leader should make every effort to teach, support, and encourage weak members.

Supportive

All members do not have the same needs, personalities, stamina, level of spirituality, and ability. Therefore, each member must be treated as an individual with decency, patience, in Christian love, and true concern for his or her welfare.

Many will come from other religious administrations with which they are familiar where things were done "differently" from what you are presenting. A new environment may cause them to become subdued or even lost depending on the climate of the group. It is therefore important to encourage them in holiness, daily prayer, fasting, attending Sunday School and other times for Bible study.

Merely encouraging members to attend church regularly is not enough. Some members need more than being in a church. They need relationship, belongingness, inclusion, and love. Each member needs to know of his or her importance and that there is interest shown in being a member of the group.

Fairness

According to David, *"He that rules over men [must] be just, ruling in the fear of God. And [he shall be] as the light of the morning, [when] the sun rises, [even] a morning without clouds; [as] the tender grass [springing] out of the earth by clear shining after rain"* (II Samuel 23:3-4).

It may seem difficult at times to treat each person with fairness because of personality differences and other factors. However, the passage above says it all in terms of the blessings which follow the leader who is fair to all.

Fairness means that even when there is time for confrontation (Matthew 18:15); or correction (II Timothy 3:16); these will be done in love (Ephesians 4:15); and not in the flesh (II Corinthians 10:3). It also means being respectful to members and treating adults as adults and children accordingly.

10

Conducting Meetings

Meetings are called to receive and to give information, and to find out what is going on in the different ministries. It is a time when feedback is given and people are allowed to express themselves about things in their lives or get information concerning the church. At the start of the meeting, the leader must produce the rules for its procedure and the conduct of members.

Suggestions for the Procedure of Meetings

1. Give advance notice concerning purpose, date, time, and place, and who should attend.
2. Make adequate preparations for the meeting including an agenda.
3. Begin on time by showing respect for other peoples' time.
4. Note different personalities, needs, and communication skills.
5. Be quick to explain and give solutions and reasons.
6. Keep the procedures spiritual and professional.
7. Observe proper order for the meeting and do not allow discussions to get out of hand.
8. Curb outbursts early and remind members of the rules.
9. Be respectful to the members and respond to questions.
10. Always seek to get everyone involved and give opportunities for each member to express grievances, and problems.
11. Be present in the meeting. Pay attention and listen carefully.
12. Keep excellent records and follow meeting procedures.
13. Leave room for other items that are not on the agenda.
14. Be gentle and kind with wisdom, patience, and understanding.
15. Before closing ask if anyone is in doubt concerning the discussions. Do not assume that everyone understood everything.
16. Set the date for the next meeting.

Important Points

1. It is important to let those who work closely with you, know how they are doing. For example: the Sunday School Teacher, Youth Leader and others.
2. Always temper error with mercy and kindness.
3. Make sure the discipline is timely and that it fits the situation.
4. Encourage to promote growth and development.
5. Do not discipline in the presence of others.
6. Be sensitive to the other person's feelings.
7. Do not use your position to put down another person.
8. Feedback must be used
   a. to bring about change
   b. to improve, and develop policies and procedures
   c. for the benefit and success of everyone,
   d. for correction,
   e. for the mission of the ministry.

Some Reasons Why Members do not attend Meetings

1. If you are not organized people will not want to show up at your meeting.
2. If you are unprepared and without an agenda you will face chaos, and the members will not respect you.
3. Members' time is precious and they do not want a drawn out meaningless meeting.
4. If there is favouritism where you allow some individuals to speak out while others are ignored or reprimanded, you will lose respect.
5. If you do not adhere to the rules you set you will lose support.
6. You do not set effective examples or stick to your own plans.

Part II
Dealing with Conflict

11

Conflict

Conflict is a disagreement between parties, or it could be individual internal struggles. It is inevitable in all human interactions and often develops because we relate with people who are often different with varying types of opinions, values, goals, beliefs, desires and needs. The resolution of those differences depends on whether people are willing to take advice, forgive offenses, and change destructive behaviours. The leader must be aware that conflict is a natural everyday occurrence, and it is inescapable in all human social activities.

Different Types of Conflict

Conflict can be positive or negative and these are demonstrated either within oneself (*intra-psychic*) or between parties (*interpersonal*).

There is also *intra-group* conflict that sometimes occurs when there are personal interests and unmet needs within the group.

Inter-group conflict is between groups, e.g. one church against another; different ministries and departments.

Categories of Conflict
Constructive Conflict

When conflict occurs in the church or group it is not a bad thing if it is handled carefully and dealt with in a Christian manner. Moreover, conflict can be valuable because it allows people to present different viewpoints and to express themselves. Conflict is constructive when people are able to express themselves because it relieves stress, anxiety and emotions. Furthermore, the presence of conflict can be a sign of problems and the way it is dealt with will help to build better understanding and problem solving skills.

Many times when conflict occurs, it becomes spiritualized and is considered to be the work of the devil. It is true that Satan is the root of many of our problems, but I believe that he gets too many credits when problems arise in human interactions.

Conflict is with us daily making it difficult to escape some of the times. There are conflicts within [intra-psychic] and conflicts without [interpersonal]. The leader deals with conflicts by turning to the word. For *internal conflict* (Psalm 55:22; I Peter 5:7). *Interpersonal conflict* (Psalm 5:11; Matthew 5:23-24; Philippians 2; 4:6-8).

Destructive Conflict

Despite its positive side, conflict can be destructive and evil when one person hides an offence, pretending that a problem does not exist. This behaviour results in anger, resentment, and hostility. Another way in which conflict becomes destructive is when the dissenting parties avoid confrontation or compromise a wrong. If the presence of conflict takes attention away from other important activities or undermines morale or self-concept this will escalate and cause destructive behaviours.

In addition, if people and groups are polarized this course of action forms a barrier and causes resentment. Destructive conflict leads to irresponsible and harmful behaviours, such as in-fighting, name-calling, back-biting and so on. Also, when people run away to escape confrontation, these are behaviours that will eventually escalate into fully blown conflict. One of the major causes for conflict in a group is weak leadership skills. This will create discouragement and hostilities if the leader does not try to resolve problems in a timely manner.

The Nature of Conflict

1. Conflict can be positive, healthy, and productive for a group. If people express their feelings and needs in a positive and constructive way, it reduces anxiety and prevents escalation of problems.
2. However, when people do not or are unable to express themselves because of environmental climatic conditions, this can result in conflict.
3. Conflict can be negative depending on how it is handled.
4. Conflict is inevitable. We meet it every day.

Advantages of Conflict

1. The occurrence of conflict can be a way of resolving differences and responding to issues that are causing tension between group members.
2. Conflict can create innovation and direct the group in ways that members would not have anticipated earlier.

Disadvantages of Conflict

1. However, conflict can tear a group apart, thus increasing tension among members.
2. Conflict can break relationships.
3. It can be costly in terms of time and money.

Some Reasons for Conflict

Interpersonal conflict may be the cause of envy and jealousies – James 3:14-16. It can also be a form of self-glory. In addition, poor communication skills and mixed messages from leaders to members will result in conflict situations.

Internal or intra-psychic conflict will result in discouragement – I Samuel 30:6; Jeremiah 20; personal sorrows and affliction.

Emotional situations will create the environment for destructive conflict resulting in discord, lack of self-control, disobedience, destructive anger, compromise, competitiveness, whispering, gossiping, unforgiving spirit, and backbiting.

Other Reasons include the following:

1. When expectations are not stated from the very beginning.
2. Misunderstanding of what is expected from each member.
3. When members are having difficulty scheduling meetings.
4. Lack of clear principles and rules.
5. Disrespect for authority and for one another.
6. Poor communication skills.
7. Lack of commitment to the common goal.
8. Personal agenda and self-centredness.

Methods for Dealing with Conflict

Seek Peace

"Blessed [are] the peacemakers; for they shall be called the children of God" (Matthew 5:9). When trying to resolve a conflict situation, it is important to work toward a "win-win resolution." The Bible teaches, *"...Seek peace and pursue it"* [Psalm 34:14b].

Compromise

1. This strategy emphasizes both parties giving up something they want in order to reach an amicable outcome. It is a good method when parties are willing to listen to each other.

2. Facilitator talks with disputing members separately [caucus] to isolate misunderstandings, and then bring the two members together to work out their differences.

Mediation

1. This is a voluntary method, requiring a third neutral party to assist the members in reaching an agreement.
2. The facilitator in mediation assumes that the parties know their positions, and their needs. This enables them to come up with their own solution.
3. Listen attentively and allow each person the same length of time to speak.
4. Insist upon the parties that they follow the procedures for the discussion.
5. Maintain trust with objectivity and get the disputants to communicate. This may be the first time they are talking since the dispute.
6. When trying to resolve a situation, focus on things you can change.
7. You cannot change someone's beliefs or values; but you can change tasks or plans.

Review

1. Describe some conflict situations you were faced with. How did you handle the incident?
2. What advice would you give to a member who has problems with another one and who decides that she will no longer speak to the offender?
3. How would you deal with a member who openly disrespects you?
4. What will you do if a member lied on you?
5. What would you do if another leader accuses you of mismanagement of the ministry which does not include finance?

12

The Systematic Features of Conflict

Conflict is a systematic situation which begins with an *event* whatever it might be. The injured person may be hurt *emotions* [affective], and decides to take *action* [behavioural] to show how he feels. He then evaluates the incident [*thoughts* cognitive] and feelings to decide how to respond to the incident.

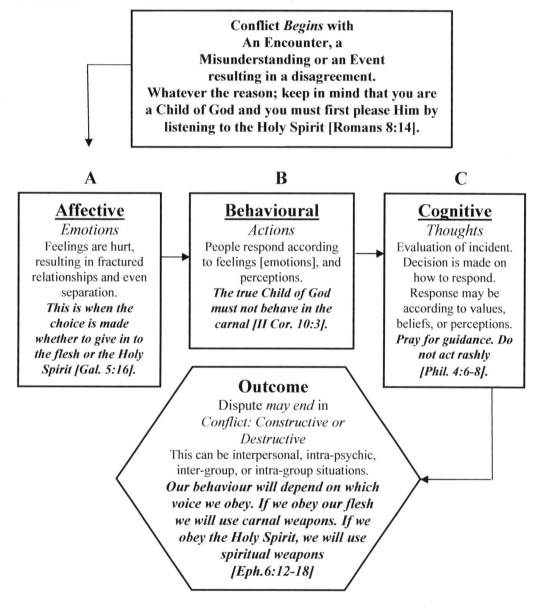

**Conflict *Begins* with
An Encounter, a
Misunderstanding or an Event
resulting in a disagreement.
Whatever the reason; keep in mind that you are
a Child of God and you must first please Him by
listening to the Holy Spirit [Romans 8:14].**

A

B

C

Affective
Emotions
Feelings are hurt, resulting in fractured relationships and even separation.
This is when the choice is made whether to give in to the flesh or the Holy Spirit [Gal. 5:16].

Behavioural
Actions
People respond according to feelings [emotions], and perceptions.
The true Child of God must not behave in the carnal [II Cor. 10:3].

Cognitive
Thoughts
Evaluation of incident. Decision is made on how to respond. Response may be according to values, beliefs, or perceptions.
Pray for guidance. Do not act rashly [Phil. 4:6-8].

Outcome
Dispute *may end* in
Conflict: Constructive or Destructive
This can be interpersonal, intra-psychic, inter-group, or intra-group situations.
Our behaviour will depend on which voice we obey. If we obey our flesh we will use carnal weapons. If we obey the Holy Spirit, we will use spiritual weapons [Eph.6:12-18]

13

Conflict Management

Conflict is not new, but has been around since the beginning of time. No matter how hard we try, there will be times when we and others do not agree because of personal differences in values, opinions, cultural, economic, and educational backgrounds.

Nevertheless, conflict of itself is harmless. It is the way it is managed, that makes conflict destructive. There are many situations that will cause conflict among members, and the leader must be very astute, and work with the wisdom of the Holy Spirit when trying to resolve those events.

Situations that Cause Problems

Leader vs. member: leaders sometimes talk down to members from the pulpit, which is a sign of cowardice, insecurity and lack of faith in God. When those situations occur, the leader has poor communication and interpersonal skills, and lacks deportment, and respect for members.

Member vs. member: holding grudges and resentment from past hurts, unforgiveness, and envy.

Member vs. leader: when members show lack of respect and trust, blaming, refusal to work in the church, holding on to grudges and resentment. Legalism, autocracy, and selfishness in leaders will lead to indifference from members and cause division.

Jealousy, covetousness: member to member; leader to leader.

Poor interpersonal relationship: hard to get along with others, one-man band, no delegating.

Opposition from members and other leaders who believe they can do a better job. Usually, beneath the grumblings one will find envy and jealousies. It happens all the time.

Lack of integrity: untrustworthiness, unreliability, inconsistency

Intra-psychic conflict: personal problems, fear, and when personal needs are not met, misunderstandings and miscommunication

Lack of respect: your values are not appreciated

Your personality is under attack: people judge you, and question your training, qualifications, experience, and knowledge of leadership

Your cultural background is under attack

Positive Conflict Management

Effective listening (James 1:19)

1. Attention – being present
2. Body language - attitude
3. Empathy – sensitivity
4. Respect – deportment
5. Reflection – ask questions for explanation

Confronting (Matthew 18:15-17).

1. Prayer
2. Privacy
3. Timing
4. Place
5. Attitude
6. Working through problems together

Employing the Holy Spirit

To receive power to overcome and resist temptation.

Trust in God

Allowing God to defend you when you do not know what to do.

Forgiveness instead of retaliation

You can let go, and move on without bitterness.

Prayer

Pray about the situation and for the offender.

Negative Conflict Management

1. *Avoidance*: Running away, pretending, lies, malice, and hypocrisy.
2. *Individualizing*: Focusing on the person who caused the problem, rather than on the issues.
3. *Emotional*: Anger and blaming others without trying to discuss the issues.
4. *Competitiveness*: Looking out for oneself by promoting a win/lose solution.
5. *Inattentiveness*: Poor communication, lack of commitment.
6. *Disrespect*: Casting insults, slurs, innuendoes, and refusing to listen.
7. *Slander*: Gossiping about the offender and spreading rumours.
8. *Unforgiving*: Revenge, animosities, grudges, hostility, unrelenting.
9. *Accommodating*: Accepting anything to avoid confrontation.
10. *Passivity and fear*: Not speaking up.

Review

1. Give an example of a positive conflict situation which you resolved amicably.
2. Give an example of a negative conflict situation which went out of hand.
    a. How did you manage the dispute?
    b. Is the dispute still going on?
    c. What was the outcome?
    d. What lessons did you learn from both the positive and the negative dispute?
3. Why is effective listening so important in a dispute?
4. Why do you think a simple disagreement can turn out to be destructive conflict?

14

Personal Conflict Resolution Strategies

1. *Seek peace* [Abigail] – I Samuel 25, [Abraham] (Genesis 13:7-9)

2. *Being Respectful* II Samuel 12

3. *Forgiveness* Genesis 50:19-21

4. *Controlling your anger* Colossians 4:6; Ephesians 4:26

5. *Speaking the truth in love* Ephesians 4:15

6. *Not revealing secrets Proverbs* 21:23; 25:15; 18:21; James 3

7. *Choosing the right words* Proverbs 15:1

8. *Patience – wait upon the Lord* Psalm 55:22, Proverbs 20:22

9. *Without partiality* Proverbs 28:21; 18:5; Romans 13:7

10. *Without toxins of hatred, malice, envy, pride, and gossip* Colossians 3:8, 9; Galatians 5:20-21

11. *Being honest* Proverbs 28:23

12. *With humility* I Peter 5:6

13. *Loving others as yourself* I Corinthians 13:4-7

14. *Walking in the Spirit* Galatians 5:16, 22-25

15. *Use of Spiritual weapons* Ephesians 6:12-18

15

Four-Step Conflict Resolution based on Wisdom

"But the wisdom that is from above is first pure, then peaceable, gentle, and easy to be entreated, full of mercy and good fruits, without partiality, and without hypocrisy" (James 3:17).

The leader must have a plan to manage conflict when it arises in the church. An effective leader will recognize and encourage the gifts in the church as a conflict management method in order to remain in the will of the Lord, and not give place to the enemy. The four-step process includes the following:

- Confrontation
- Questioning
- Effective Listening
- Resolution

Confrontation

(a) **Wisdom** *is pure, peaceable, and gentle*
   1. *Pray before you* begin. Although the Bible indicates confrontation (Matthew 18:15-17], the process begins with wisdom.
   2. *Choose the right* time and a private place away from other persons who might overhear the conversation.
   3. *Ground rules* are necessary for order and direction of the meeting.
   4. *Get the facts* and find out what the dispute is about if you do not know. Before you can deal with a problem you must know what it is about; therefore, get all the facts. Be very patient, sensitive and flexible. Avoid blaming.
   5. *Act quickly* and do not allow too much time to elapse before you confront the other party concerning the issues. Observe the instructions in Ephesians 4:26: *Be ye angry, and sin not: let not the sun go down upon your wrath. Matthew 5: 23-26*

6. *Present your case without bitterness.* Paul points out in Ephesians 4:31 *Let all bitterness, and wrath, and anger, and clamour, and evil speaking be put away from you, with all malice:* Hebrews 12:15 *Looking diligently lest any man fail of the grace of God; lest any root of bitterness springing up trouble you, and thereby many be defiled.*

7. *Be respectful.* Confrontation does not mean rudeness. There must be respect and avoid being angry to the point of causing embarrassment. According to Ecclesiastes 7:9 which states, *"Be not hasty in thy spirit to be angry: for anger rests in the bosom of fools."*

Questioning

(b) Wisdom *is easily entreated [teachable, patient, submissive, and understanding]*

1. Set the tone by observing the instructions from Solomon.[4]
2. Design your questions so that they are not ambiguous or intimidating.
3. Do not use jargons and technical language unless you explain their meaning.
4. Avoid closed questions with "yes" and "no" answers.
5. Allow the individual/s to describe precisely the details of the incident.
6. Make sure that everyone understands, and give enough time for the other party to think and respond.
7. Leave room for clarification and explanation, and be present with your body language.
8. For example:
   a. "Were you there?"
   b. "What were you doing?"
9. Probe gently with open-ended questions:
   a. "Tell me more"
   b. "Why...?"
10. Describe how you felt. "What happened?" For example –
    a. "Can you explain to me if you were there, and what you were doing at the time when it happened?"

---

[4] Proverbs 15:23 *"A word fitly spoken is like apples of gold in pictures of silver." "A man hath joy by the answer of his mouth: and a word spoken in due season, how good is it!" (Proverbs* 25:11).

  b. "Is there anything more you can tell me about it?

11. Be sensitive and empathetic to the other person's feelings.

Effective Listening

(c) Wisdom *is [full of mercy and good fruits]*

1. Be attentive, thoughtful, reflective, and considerate.
2. Weigh the matter carefully and be selective, flexible, patient, respectful and empathetic.
3. Make sure you understand what is being said by asking for explanations.
4. Give feedback when appropriate.
5. Be receptive to other communication styles - summarize, clarify, reframe.
6. Be congruent with your speech and body language.
7. Avoid being judgmental

Resolution

(d) Wisdom *is [without partiality and hypocrisy]*

1. *Examine your **perception*** of the issues to find out if the conflict is
   (a) destructive
   (b) manageable or
   (c) was it inevitable
2. *Examine the **events*** which led to the problem.
   (a) When did it happen?
   (b) What caused the conflict to happen?
   (c) Who are the people involved?
   (d) What did each person do to cause the dispute?
3. *Discuss the **issues*** with the other party decently and orderly with the observance of the ground rules.
   (a) Give your undivided attention while the other person is speaking.
   (b) Be tactful, yet discreet.
   (c) Explain your position and find out what the other person wants.
   (d) Work out how the issues can be resolved
   (e) What are the interests and needs?
   (f) Decide how those needs will be met.
   (g) Decide who will do what, when, and how.
4. *Set clear, specific and reachable goals.* It is important that *everyone* understands the goals.

5. *Brainstorm to reach solutions.* Find out what are the options and select the best ones that will be feasible to the solution.
6. *Evaluate feedback* and try to reach an amicable resolution.
7. *Obtain confirmation of agreement* from each person, which can be verbal or written.
8. *Seek for Clarity* to ensure that everyone understands what each has to do to restore the relationship or fix the problem.

Situations that will prevent an amicable result

1. When there is a threat to one's self-esteem and pride.
2. If someone is defensive, tries to escape, criticizes, or lies.
3. Anger will interrupt or prevent the discussion from taking place in a peaceful environment.
4. If hurtful language is used, and remarks that will humiliate or otherwise create strife.
5. If someone is difficult and refuses to see reason.
6. An unforgiving spirit will hinder progress.

Review

1. What do you do when conflicts arise in the church?
2. What are your ideas concerning the development of conflicts in the church?
3. Describe conflicts in the early church and how they were resolved?
4. Do you see the same situations in the local church?
5. What causes conflict among believers or churches?
6. How can you be a peacemaker in a conflict situation?
7. What are some positive conflict situations you have experienced?
8. What are some negative conflict situations you have experienced?
9. When is conflict good or bad? Explain.

16

Other Suggestions for Reducing Conflict

There are Scriptures which are effective for conflict resolution

1. Try to keep calm when everyone else is getting upset.

2. Take a walk.

3. Do something to avoid being drawn into strife.

4. If you can talk with the person/s, do so.

5. Always endeavour to maintain the peace of God in your heart with a song, a word, or some special point from a message.

6. Seek for wholeness and not division.

7. Do not condone sin.

8. Use wisdom in your interactions especially with a troublesome person.

9. Be kind towards everyone and show respect.

10. Do all in your power to avoid strife and do not be overtaken by it.

11. Be compassionate.

12. Practice forgiving others and yourself when you have done wrong.

13. Do not hold grudges, this will erode the grace of God in you.

14. Do not respond to everything that is said about you.

15. Do not react to situations; instead be proactive.

16. Be kind and gentle to everyone as much as you are able.

17. Show that you are a peacemaker by your behaviour.

18. Be willing to give up your rights, and allow God to fight for you.

19. Do not show off when you have a gift or can do more than others can.

20. Do not use your position, ability, ministry, talent as a weapon.

21. Do not entertain gossip.

22. Be sure of facts.

23. Do not slander anyone or spread rumours.

24. Practice self-control.

25. Let your speech be with grace, seasoned with salt.

26. Do not dispute over differences of opinion about religion/denomination.

27. Be honest with your opinions.

28. Avoid hidden agendas.

29. Be a good example of Christian character and discipline.

30. Ask God to help you to control your tongue.

31. Let someone see the Lord Jesus in you.

17

Problem Solving Strategies

Do not try to solve a problem without first following these steps.

1. Identify the problem

2. Separate the issues from the individual

3. Attack the problem/issue and not the individual

4. Be clear about how you feel towards the situation

5. Be specific, sincere and honest

6. Respect each other

7. Present needs with precise descriptions

8. Describe your part

9. Express your approval/disapproval concerning the issue with sincerity

10. Listen and communicate effectively

11. Avoid mixed messages

12. Do not criticize or call the other person insulting names

13. Look at options for resolution - search for alternatives

14. Aim for solutions based on needs/interests rather than solutions

15. Do not base your strategy on assumptions

16. Identify the problem before finding a solution

17. Do not attack the individual

18. Be clear about how you feel towards the situation

19. Brainstorm for options for resolution.

20. Seek for feedback and make changes where needed.

18

Scriptures for Dealing with Problems

1. *Attitudes and behaviours*: Philippians 2:5-7.

2. *Building Christian character*, *conduct*, and *positive thinking*: Philippians 4:8.

3. *Truthfulness*: Psalm 15:2; Zechariah 8:16; Ephesians 4:15, 25;

4. *Encouraging Collaboration and unity*: Philippians 2:2-7.

5. *Encouraging Effective Interpersonal Relationship*: Philippians 2:3-4.

6. *Confrontation*: Matthew 18:15-17.

7. *Compromise*: Nehemiah 6:1-4.

8. *Dealing with Slander*: Nehemiah 6:5-9.

9. *Dealing with Anger [Self or Others]*: Proverbs 14:29; 15:18; 17:27; Ecclesiastics 7:9; Ephesians 4:47; James 1:19.

10. *An unforgiving spirit*: Matthew 18; Mark 11:25, 26.

11. *Creating an Environment of Peace*: Psalm 34:13, 14; Matthew 5:9.

19

Communication and Conflict

Effective communication is one of the most important elements in management. If leaders do not express themselves effectively it will cause problems such as animosities and hostilities in the church. Always remember that other people cannot read your mind.

Examples of Ineffective Listening
1. You interrupt or jump to conclusions before a person has finished speaking;
2. You concentrate on our own responses in an attempt to attack the speaker;
3. You go off on mental tangents and totally ignore the speaker;
4. You fidget and look bored;
5. You show open disgust and lack of respect;
6. You fall asleep or read a book rather than listen to the speaker;
7. You do not show interest.

Examples of Effective Listening

1. You concentrate on what the person is saying rather than anything about the individual – looks, dress, etc.;
2. You listen with an open mind rather than assuming that the person speaking is wrong or uninformed;
3. You focus on the ways in which you agree with the speaker rather than the ways you disagree;
4. You provide the speaker with positive feedback to encourage;
5. You show interest with being present by your body language;
6. Reflect, and interpret what the speaker says;
7. You show respect;
8. You sit upright and do not slouch in your chair;
9. You ask pertinent questions and smile;
10. You thank the speaker at the end of the session.

Listening Tips

1. Try to make eye contact [body language]
2. Do not interrupt
3. Always lean forward and show interest
4. Do not attempt to finish what the other person is saying
5. Be congruent with your body language
6. Pay attention to the speaker
7. Give compliments, especially pointing out points of interests

Conflict Terminologies

1. *Avoidance*: escape, non-confrontation
2. *Competitive*: win/lose, rivalry
3. *Compromise*: looking for the easy way out, carelessness, neglect
4. *Accommodating*: not willing to discuss; accepting to keep the peace
5. *Collaborate*: discussion, unity, problem-solving

Reactions to Conflict

There are many reactions that are used to escalate conflict

1. *Body language* makes a significant impression
   a. <u>Facial expressions</u>: frowning, winking of the eye
   b. <u>Inattentiveness</u>: yawning, reading, writing, distractions
   c. <u>Posture</u>: folding of the arms, slouching, hissing
   d. <u>Talking</u>: causing disruption, snickering
   e. <u>Projection</u> – blame, lying
2. *Cover up* – stork-like, sweeping under the carpet
3. *Pretend* - unwilling to admit
4. *Anger* – accusing, attacking, shouting
5. *Name calling* - insults, innuendoes
6. *Gossiping* - telling everybody
7. *Reacting* - making a scene

What is Your Approach to Conflict as a Christian Leader?

1. What if your personal values and beliefs are not compatible to those of the other party?
2. How do show objectivity and fairness
3. In a conflict situation, how do you conduct your behaviour/
4. What kinds of language do you use?
5. What is your tone and attitude like?
6. How do you deal with diversities such as
    a. different religious beliefs,
    b. cultural differences,
    c. language barriers, and
    d. differing communication styles?

Review

1. What are your ideas about conflict?
2. Do you view conflict as an opportunity
    a. For change;
    b. For Introspection;
    c. For Personal/organizational growth;
    d. For Personal Awareness?
3. What are your perceptions?
4. How do you feel about conflict when it happens?
5. What is your understanding of conflict?
    a. Are you a facilitator;
    b. Provider of solutions;
    c. An agent of change;
    d. Problem fixer?

20

Conflict Situations Role Plays

These are from real-life situations. Some of the information has been changed.

1. You are a Sunday Bible School Teacher and the person who usually gives out the books is out of town. When you became a member you were told that only regular students were given books.

   You received books for the next quarter when a member who is a known troublemaker, and seldom attends asks you for a copy. You told the person that the books were only for regular members and politely asked: "Are you going to attend regularly." The person took an offence and started an argument. To avoid further dispute you gave the individual a book. Minutes later she came back and shoved it into your hands in front of another individual.

   It is Sunday morning and service is about to begin. The same day you were later called into question, only to be told by the offended in the presence of others that for seven months she had not forgiven you about a misunderstanding. How will you deal with this situation?

2. One day at work you were standing next to your supervisor in the presence of a class of about fifteen persons. You were responsible for ordering the refreshments for the workshop and ordered what you were told. However, it turned out that she should have told you to order another item. She argued with you in the presence of the entire group about the shortness of food, which you knew was not your fault. Without warning, she said very sternly "next time order that item" as if you were the one to blame. Describe how you would deal with this situation.

3. You were present at church when one of the leaders asked to see you. To your surprise you have been charged with having an affair with one of the

members in the church. There is no such truth in this story. Describe what you would do.

4. You have been a member of your church for almost five years. There was going to be a function by a family in the church and you heard that nearly everyone was invited but you were not. A few days before the event took place a family member stopped you after church and said "Oh, we are having a celebration on Saturday but you were not sent an invitation because your name is not in the church's computer data base." You are a regular consistent member. You pay your tithes with a willingness to do anything in the church. What would you do in such a situation as this?

5. Rumour has it that you have chased a member out of the student school class. There is no such truth in it. What would you do?

6. You are in church one night and in the testimony service someone got up and said derogatory things about you. What would you do?

7. You were in church and one of the leaders' wives wrongfully accuses you in the presence of everyone. What would you do?

8. You are at your job and a leaders' wife called you and abused you in a threatening manner over the phone. Later in the week you received messages on the job and at home declaring you to be a troublemaker and mischievous. You are not guilty of any such accusations. What would you do?

Part III

Biblical Leadership Styles

21

The Leadership of Jesus

The Perfect Example

It is not possible to find any imperfections with the manner in which Jesus demonstrated leadership with His disciples. He did not leave them in any doubt concerning love, servant-hood, humility, sincerity, and all the necessary qualities required for effective spiritual leadership.

In reviewing Jesus' leadership style, it is clear to see that He was the *fountain* of hope for the hopeless. He was the *healer* of broken hearts, and *restorer* to the weary. Those who seemed lost could find *refuge* in Him, and He brought *joy* to the cheerless. Moreover, He gave *peace* to the confused, and *faith* to the distraught.

Servant-hood
Although Jesus was the Son of God, yet He lived a life of servant-hood by giving of Himself to the needs of others. He never saw any task too menial for Him to perform when someone had a need. Without thinking of Himself, He would rather feel hunger so that He could meet with a woman in Samaria who was in need of Salvation (John 4).

Jesus was the perfect servant leader, and this was demonstrated at the last Supper with His disciples (Mark 13:4-14). I do not believe the example of washing their feet was for them to carry out this procedure each time they met.

The lesson of feet-washing was to teach that as His servants, there will be times when they might be faced with situations that will test their spirituality and loyalty to Him.

Jesus showed the Disciples how to deal with tasks which may not seem integral to their definition of leadership; but will demonstrate humility and love as His servants.

Therefore, rather than preach humility to the Disciples, Jesus showed them by His own example.

The example was also an indication that there are all kinds of people whom we will meet with different types of personalities and needs. For this reason there will be times when leaders will have to make adjustments in their own positions, maybe as a pastor to do even the lowest of tasks for the Kingdom of God.

Jesus wanted his disciples to recognize that effective spiritual leadership requires true love for the people who are being led.

Jesus further indicated: *"Ye know that the princes of the Gentiles exercise dominion over them...But it shall not be so among you; but whosoever will be great among you, let him be your minister; And whosoever will be chief among you, let him be your servant: Even as the Son of man came not to be ministered unto, but to minister, and to give his life a ransom for many"* (Matthew 20:25b-28).

Moreover, Paul instructed all leaders to *"Take heed therefore unto yourselves, and to all the flock, over the which the Holy Ghost hath made you overseers, to feed the church of God, which he hath purchased with his own blood"* (Acts 20:28). Those leaders who are negligent or have abdicated their responsibilities for service, God will judge severely [James 3:1], and He is no respect of persons.

Role Model

After Jesus had washed His disciples' feet, He said: *"If I then, [your] Lord and Master, have washed your feet; ye also ought to wash one another's feet. For I have given you an example, that ye should do as I have done to you"* (John 13:14-15).

Another illustration was when Jesus included Judas at the Last Supper, who would have soon betrayed Him. While he administered to the other disciples, He also served Judas. This was indeed a great example to follow in treating those who hurt and humiliate us. This calls for great grace and courage under the inspiration of the Holy Spirit.

Humility

Jesus demonstrated true humility when He laid His life down for the sins of mankind. Although He had no sin and did no wrong, yet, He was treated as a common criminal because of His willingness to be obedient to the Father and to fulfill the plan for Salvation.

This obedience meant the shedding of His blood because this is the only one God would accept to redeem mankind from eternal death, and separation from His presence.

According to the word: *"And almost all things are by the law purged with blood: and without shedding of blood is no remission"* (Hebrews 9:22).

Paul reflected on Jesus' manifestation of humility with encouragement of:
"Let this mind be in you, which was also in Christ Jesus: Who, being in the form of God, thought it not robbery to be equal with God: But made himself of no reputation, and took on the form of a servant, and was made in the likeness of men: And being found in fashion as a man, he humbled himself, and became obedient unto death, even the death of the cross" (Philippians 2:5-8).

The spiritual leader must be clothed with the adornment of humility in order to please God.

Review

1. If you were Jesus, how would you have treated Judas?
2. What does it mean to be humble in this day where most people are selfish and self-opinionated even in the church community?
3. Does humility counts anymore?
4. Are you a role model for emulation?
5. Are you a servant-leader for Jesus Christ?

22
Moses
The Humble Leader

Moses is an example of accepting sound advice when his father-in-law observed that his leadership style was not working. Moses' acceptance reflects a humble spirit and a willingness to listen. He took the advice and changed his style by delegating to other honourable men. (*See* Exodus 18).

He was Meek and Forgiving

(Numbers 12:1-3) *Miriam and Aaron spake against Moses because of the Ethiopian woman whom he had married... (Now the man Moses was very meek, above all the men which were upon the face of the earth.)*

And Aaron said unto Moses, Alas, my lord, I beseech thee, lay not the sin upon us, wherein we have done foolishly, and where we have sinned.

And Moses cried unto the Lord, saying, **Heal her now, O God, I beseech thee** [vv. 11-13

He took his Responsibilities seriously

[He sent men out to spy out the land – investigate the land, Numbers 13].

He stood against rebellion and insults (Numbers 14:2-4), *And all the people murmured against Moses and against Aaron...And they said one to another, Let us make a captain, and let us return to Egypt.*

He was an Intercessor
[Numbers 14:11-19].

He bargained with God for the people and stood between God's judgment and them.

And the Lord said unto Moses, How long will this people provoke me?...I will smite them with the pestilence, and disinherit them, and will make of thee a greater nation and mightier than they.

Verse 13.

And Moses said unto the Lord, Then the Egyptians shall hear it, (for thou broughtest up this people in thy might from among them. ...

Verse 15:

Now if thou shalt kill <u>all</u> this people as one man, then the nations which have heard the fame of thee will speak saying, Because the Lord was not able to bring this people into the land which he sware unto them, therefore he hath slain them in the wilderness.

Exodus 32:30-35

Moses said unto the people, Ye have sinned a great sin: and now I will go up unto the Lord; peradventure I shall make an atonement for your sin...

He put his life on the line, *Yet now, if thou wilt forgive their sin-; and if not, blot me, I pray thee out of thy book which thou hast written.*

He had an Intimate Relationship with God

Exodus 33:11

And the Lord spake unto Moses face to face, as a man speaks unto his friend... God was his leader and he had a personal relationship with Him.

Delegate
Exodus 18:13-27

And when Moses' father-in-law saw all that he did to the people, he said, What is this thing that thou doest to thyself alone, and all the people stand by thee from morning unto even? He was willing to listen to good advice to delegate and spread the tasks.

He sought God's presence and trusted him
Exodus 33:15-17

And he said if thy presence go not with me, carry us not up hence...and the Lord said unto Moses, I will do this thing also that thou hast spoken: for thou has found grace in my sight, and I know thee by name

He was Emotional
Numbers 20:7-13

...And he said unto them... Hear now, ye rebels; must we fetch you water out of this rock? He was angry and struck the rock instead of speaking to it as God commanded him

He was a man of Prayer

Several times he prayed for the people and even put his own life on the line for them.

Review

1. Do you think Moses was a soft person?
2. Should Moses have given up on those unthankful people?
3. Why do you think he put his soul on the line for people who were so disobedient and forgetful of God's mercies and love?
4. What would you have done if you were in his place?
5. How are you coping with intractable members?

23

Eli

The Complacent Leader

Eli seemed to have been the type of leader who was calm and unruffled even though he tried to reprimand his sons for their evil doing. His children did not follow the law, but did whatever they wanted with no regard for godliness or even morality.

Clearly, they did not fear nor obey God and had no respect for their father or the position he held. When God decided to take action against Eli's house his response was *"It is the Lord: let him do what seemeth him good"* (I Samuel 3:18b). He was obviously untroubled concerning God's plan for the destruction of his house.

At that point the Bible does not state whether Eli interceded for his children, nor did he show any emotion. It is possible that he had been embarrassed by the sins of his sons. This makes one ask the question "What can a pastor do about unsaved children who ignore the gospel?" My answer to this is to keep on praying and interceding. Never give up.

Lack of Discernment

> I Samuel 1:14 *How long wilt thou be drunken? Put away thy wine from thee. He was spiritually blind and could not see that Hanna was in great sorrow.*

Eli's household

1. *Now the sons of Eli [were] sons of Belial; they knew not the Lord* (I Samuel 2:1). They did not obey the Lord nor fear Him.

2. If a leader cannot control his/her own family, that person is hardly fit to lead the people of God.

3. What is God looking for in a leader? *One that rules well his own house, having his children in subjection with all gravity. For if a man know not how to rule his own house, how shall he take care of the church of God?* I Timothy 3:4.

The Replacement

1. If as leaders we fail to carry out our duties, God will raise up someone in our place.

2. Eli *was very old, and heard all that his sons did unto all Israel...* (I Samuel 2:22f), it would appear that this was the time he tried to scold his sons, who were grown men and had wives of their own. If, as a leader you do not keep checks and control with feedback, you will be held responsible for your negligence.

3. God used a young child to warn the priest about his leadership duties and responsibilities and to inform him that he would be replaced.

Going through the Motions

1. Eli no longer heard from God. In I Samuel 3, after God called Samuel and spoke to him he reported to Eli whose response was *"...It is the Lord: let him do what seemeth him good"* (I Samuel 3:18).

2. God will keep His word. If we do His work halfheartedly, we will suffer in some way or another. Eli and his two sons died in one day.

3. Worse still, the Ark of the Lord was taken by the enemy.

Be careful how you carry out your duties as a Leader. God is watching; and He will judge.

Review

1. How would you describe your leadership skills in comparison to Eli's?
2. What would you do if your children did not obey you?
3. At what age would you begin to correct your children when you find they are straying?

24

Joshua

A Courageous Leader

After the death of Moses, Joshua was selected to continue the work of leading the people of Israel to the Promised Land as God had directed (Joshua 1). Joshua had seen the behaviours of the people and the way they treated his predecessor Moses. Undoubtedly as a younger man, there might have been trepidation and fear, unease, and the threat of failure. Nevertheless, God was with him and encouraged him all the way.

Noticeably, one of the human skills Joshua possessed was that of follower or servant. It is not always easy or welcome to fit into another person's position especially with problematic people.

Joshua was Moses' minister, and he did his work with integrity so that Moses delegated him to go out and lead the fight when they were under attack from their enemies [Exodus 17:8-16].

The time came that Moses was now dead and here was the commission to lead a group of unruly people who was ungrateful, with constant complaining, and murmurings against God who took them out of bondage (I Corinthians 10:5-11). What could any person do better than the one who was before him? How could he bring some measure of contentment so that the people would be stable and committed to serve God in spirit and in truth? Clearly, if Moses could not settle them, what could Joshua do better?

God never leave us to struggle on our own. He gave Joshua specific encouragement to arise and go over this *Jordan, thou, and all this people, unto the land which I do give to them, even to the children of Israel. Every place that the sole of your foot shall tread upon, that I have given unto you, as I said unto*

Moses…as I was with Moses, so I will be with thee…Only be thou strong and very courageous…" (Joshua 1:1-9).

At the very beginning of his ministry, Joshua was faced with an obstacle, the river Jordan. God who is ever present encouraged him to move forward similar to how He instructed Moses to go forward towards the Red Sea.

Courage to lead means having moral fibre, fortitude, fearlessness, and boldness to face challenges and oppositions. Not everyone is born to be a leader, nor can everyone lead. To lead also means a determination to stand when facing the isolation of being alone, and or insecurity.

Joshua seemed to have been facing some kind of insecurity. Nevertheless, God encouraged him several times in the book named after him. Out of the passage (Joshua 1:1-10) we can extract a number of themes pertaining to leadership relating to courage. [See the next chapter].

Review

1. What would you do first if you had to take over from a celebrated leader?

2. How would you go about winning the hearts of people who are intractable?

3. What skills do you need to govern and guide unthankful and disobedient members?

4. How would you encourage someone who came to you about unruly members in the church?

5. How would you deal with unruly members in your church?

6. What if the unruly is your kin – wife, sibling, or parent?

7. What if the unruly member is your friend or enemy?

25

Themes on Courage

Courage to Lead: II Timothy 2:15; 4:5; James 1:19

The leader must endeavour to stand for the truth of God's word no matter what the cost. He must not water-down the gospel because God will hold him accountable for leading His people astray. It is important to study the Word and ask the Holy Spirit for the true and unadulterated interpretation.

The leader must listen to the Holy Spirit for the truths of the Word and impart this knowledge to the people. His example of submitting to the Word will enable the people to be obedient. The leader's faithfulness is not only teaching or hearing the Word, but also modeling what he teaches.

The aim of the leader is to maintain a good conscience before God. Courage to lead further means you will experience persecutions because you cannot please everyone. There will be oppositions because of different needs and differences in personalities.

The Importance of your Position: Joshua 7-8; I Timothy 6:11

You must acknowledge that your dependence is upon God. Therefore, you must rely on Him for knowledge, understanding, and wisdom, to guide, direct, and show you what to do and how to lead.

Do not rely on your intellectual ability, personality, or any exterior situations to be your support. Your strength comes from the Lord. You need His presence in everything you do, especially when making decisions and dealing with conflict.

Without God's help, you will not make it successfully. Consequently, you must study the word daily (Colossians 3:16). Do not use your position to be arrogant towards God's people. Rather, be faithful, loving, kind, patient, and meek. Your disposition must be even-temper and with self-control.

The leader must be forgiving and not hold on to grudges. Instead, he will pardon injuries, correct faults, one without partiality, and full of grace. The effective leader must be humble and submit to the leading of the Holy Spirit [James 4:7]. If he does his work without God's help, he is heading for trouble.

Courage to Move beyond what you found: John 14:12; Proverbs *29:18*

The leader must have a vision to excel and go beyond what he/she found. When we spend time with the Lord, He reveals things to us. From those revelations, the leader is able to lead the people in the way they are to be led.

Conversely, if the leader has no time for God, he is robbing the people of new insights and ideas to better lead them. Furthermore, the leader who has a vision, who is listening to God, and who has an intimate relationship with Him, places himself in an enviable position to lead God's people and to excel.

Courage to be Fearless: II Timothy 1:7; Jeremiah 1:17-19.

God does not lead us into situations that will terrify us. He does not lead us into difficult situations and then leave us to struggle wondering what to do. When we are caught in the turmoil of life, just look to God for help.

Stand still, as Moses instructed the people [Exodus 14:13-15], without fear and see what He will do. Why fear when God is in control of your life? If God took you into some difficult pathway, then He has a plan to get you out of it. Why worry when God has everything under control.

God will give us power to overcome the trials and tests of life. He will, through His grace give us strength despite the suffering whereby we can still love Him, as we trust His promises. There are times when the leader will encounter unreasonable people who are set out to destroy him. Even then, he must not back down. Rather, he should confront the adversaries and recognize that they are instruments and agents of the enemy.

God told Jeremiah *"...gird up thy loins and arise, and speak unto them all that I command thee: be not dismayed at their faces, lest I confound thee before them"* [1:17]. If we stand for God and His principles against oppositions, He will stand with us. We have no need to fear. Oppositions can be financial, people, circumstances, external, internal problems; but we have no need to fear with God on our side.

Courage to Create Leadership Positions: I Timothy 3:1-7; 4:12b-16

The leader needs courage to create new positions. He must be led by the Holy Spirit to identify wholesome men and women who can assume those positions. He must not use his intellect alone, or be guided by favouritism. Those must not be the criteria on which to make selections in order to avoid partiality.

The leader needs wisdom that will guide him in purity, peacefulness, gentleness, and mercy especially when he has to eliminate, or say "no" to someone who holds a position or who seeks a position [*See* James 3:17]. If the leader is not disciplined and obedient to the leading of the Holy Spirit, he will make the wrong decisions and his performance will not meet up to the standards of God's principles. There will be disasters even if he has a full congregation. Having a house full does not mean good spiritual leadership skills.

There are leaders who were not called into certain positions. They only use their secular business abilities to manage spiritual affairs without the sanction of the Holy Spirit. What we find is a church of over-fed, lazy, complacent people. Many still do not know the difference between the spirits of the enemy, from the Holy Spirit. Very often in such churches, leaders are selected based on their financial abilities, elitism, nepotism, and the like.

Courage for Moral Judgment [Jude 1-25]

There are so many issues in society today, which affect the church. These are often politically controlled and the church is required to take a stand. The leader must stand by his beliefs. He must state his understanding of issues when it comes to the standards of the church and the people God has placed in his hands. He must seek to please God, who is sovereign. His word does not change. His moral judgment must be based on the principles found in the word of God, and he must take a stand against immorality and behaviours that will tarnish the biblical standards of the church.

Courage to Handle Conflicts [Matthew 18:15-17]

Listen, and be respectful, prayerful, and fair. Find out the problem before trying to fix it. Always give place for explanation.

26

Nehemiah

Single-mindedness Leadership

Nehemiah was a man of purpose, faith, trust, confidence, fearlessness, and determination. His leadership should inspire others to continue the work God has called them to do even when they are faced with opposition. Although Nehemiah was mocked and laughed at, the distraction did not cause him to tremble. Instead, he went directly to God for favour, guidance, instruction, protection and encouragement.

Every leader will be faced with problems which can sometimes be open confrontation from members. This should not cause him to panic or lose composure. The leader who cannot control his emotions will have many battles that will leave him wounded. The outcome of those battles may even scatter the people God called him to lead.

In every group there are people with different needs. Some are "special needs" members who must be fed with a spoon. Others are "spiritually lame" who find it difficult to walk according to the word. Then there are those who are "controlled by the green-eyed monster." They are envious of others who are only doing their work for the Lord. Nehemiah met with some of those persons who were jealous of what he was doing. Nevertheless, he continued with his mission and was not deterred by their taunting.

Many times altercations are born out of defiance, ignorance, lack of spirituality, personal needs, which is an over-activity of the "old man" who still (Colossians 3:5-11) resides in the life of the individual. Nehemiah had those persons who were constantly gnawing at him so that he would stop the work. Despite the negative behaviours, they did not stop him or cause him to hold up the work because of insults. Instead, he encouraged the workers to continue with one hand on the weapon and the other with the work.

Unwaveringly he did not pause even when he knew there were conspirators who were preparing to sabotage the work through slander and treachery (6:5-14). Yet, he did not let none of those things move him (Acts 20:24). He was just as determined to see the work through and did not let their plots, threats, or anything deter him from his mission. The substance of the enemies' conspiracy and antagonisms was for him to compromise with the ringleaders so that the work would not be accomplished (Nehemiah 6:1-4). Nehemiah was a man with singleness of heart. He was disciplined and well-focussed with a determination to carry out his plans.

Restoration

Moreover, Nehemiah was not only concerned with the physical work alone; but also with the spiritual condition of the people. They were in a backslidden state whereby men had married women coming from idolatry; the welfare of the priests were neglected, which caused some of them to seek work outside, rather than being provided for from the Temple. The people were not paying tithes; and there were those who were involved with extortion. Hearing all those things, Nehemiah admonished the people to return to God and convinced them to obey the principles of the law. He was on a mission, and he had to see it done completely and not half-heatedly. His attitude towards his work brought repentance among the people and restoration.

Nehemiah's Traits include the following:

1. He established a reasonable and attainable goal.
2. He had a sense of mission.
3. He was willing to get involved.
4. He rearranged his priorities in order to accomplish his goal.
5. He patiently waited for God's timing.
6. He showed respect to his superior.
7. He prayed at crucial times.
8. He made his request with tact and graciousness.
9. He was well prepared and thought of his needs in advance.

10. He went through proper channels.

11. He took time (three days) to rest, pray, and plan.

12. He investigated the situation firsthand.

13. He informed others only after he knew the size of the problem.

14. He identified himself as one with the people.

15. He set a reasonable and attainable goal before the people.

16. He assured them God was in the project.

17. He displayed self-confidence in facing obstacles.

18. He displayed confidence in God in the face of obstacles.

19. He did not argue with opponents.

20. He was not discouraged by opposition.

21. He courageously used the authority of his position

27

Guidelines for Spiritual Leadership

1. Set the example for excellence and others will follow (Exodus 40:16).

2. Be an enviable example (II Thessalonians 3:9).

3. Be a servant leader (Matthew 20:26). Paul was a model servant leader (1 Thessalonians 2:1-11).

4. Do not try to do all the work by yourself, delegate (II Corinthians 6:1; Luke 9:10-50).

5. Always make every effort to instruct others (Luke 10:2-12). The most important task of the leader is the development of people.

6. Be faithful to God who called you (II Timothy 2:1-6; I Timothy 4:12-16; Titus 1:7-9; 2:7).

7. Keep a clear conscience before God and man (Acts 24:16).

8. Appoint godly workers who practice truth and who are able to communicate effectively (Titus 1:5-9).

9. Correct in love and not abrasively (I Corinthians 13).

10. Be teachable and teach by example and precepts (Titus 2).

11. Practice forgiveness and restoration (Philemon 8-16).

12. Give full attention to God's word and your relationship with Jesus (Hebrews 2:1-4).

13. Be careful with your speech (James 3).

14. Live to glorify God (1 Peter 2:12).

15. Seek to please God and not man (I Thessalonians 2:5, 6), speak the truth.

28

Nine Gifts of the Holy Spirit

[I Corinthians 12:8-10]

1. The Gift of Wisdom [v.8] – to handle disputes

1. Wisdom is the principal thing (Proverbs 4:7; better than gold, 16:16).
2. Wisdom is knowledge to understand the mysteries, doctrines, design, and nature of the gospel and the ability to explain them.
3. A word in season brings comfort (Isaiah 50:4a).

2. The Gift of Knowledge [v.8] – to teach others

1. Knowledge is supernatural revelation of information pertaining to a person or event for a specific purpose.
2. Knowledge does not come from man (II Corinthians 2:13).
3. Knowledge distinguishes between truth and falsehood.

3. The Shield of Faith [v.9; Ephesians 6] – in times of crises

1. Without faith, it is impossible to please God (Hebrews 11:6).
2. Faith is complete trust in the sovereignty, power, and mercy of God.
3. Faith means complete reliance upon God who is all wise, all-powerful, all knowing, and ever-present. A God who will not fail.

4. The Gift of Healing [v.9] – to pray for the sick

1. This is performed through faith in God by the power of the Holy Spirit.
2. Healing can be performed by the *laying of hands*; *anointing with oil*; and *prayer* (James 5:13-15) or by *the word* (Psalm 107:20; Matthew 8:8).

5. The Gift of Miracles [v.10] – to be used by God

1. These are divinely inspired, and not under the power of natural law.
2. The Bible has various examples of miracles, both in the Old and New Testaments.

6. The Gift of Prophecy [v.10] – to warn and edify others

1. This is a divine disclosure through the Holy Spirit, for edification, exhortation, and comfort of the church.
2. Prophecy is for Believers (I Corinthians 14:22b).
3. A word of caution *"The spirits of the prophet is subject to the prophets* (II Corinthians 14:32).

7. Discernment [v.10] – to know the difference the voice of the Holy Spirit and that of demons

1. To discern the spirit world
2. To understand the true motives of people
3. To understand the occurrence of circumstances
4. It is the power to distinguish between the truth and a lie (Acts 5:3, I John 4:1).
5. To know the will of God

8. Divers Tongues [v.10] – to communicate with the Lord

1. Speaking in an unknown language for worshipping and communication with God.
2. Tongues are sign to the unbelievers (I Corinthians 14:22).

9. Interpretation of Tongues [v.10] – to deliver messages from the Holy Spirit

1. This is the translation of a message from the Spirit. Usually, after more than one speaker.
2. Otherwise, the speaker is advised to keep quiet and speak to the self.

Note: these are not the only gifts in the church. See also (Romans 12:6-8; Ephesians 4:11-12

29

Personal Profile

For your Eyes Only

1. Do I view problems as opportunities?
2. Do I set priorities?
3. Am I interested in those whom I lead?
4. Do I show respect for others?
5. Am I even-tempered?
6. Am I courageous?
7. Am I a critical and creative thinker?
8. Am I committed to innovations that are best for the group?
9. Do I debate, clarify, and enunciate my values and beliefs?
10. Can I communicate at all levels?
11. Do I recognize the problems in a dispute and address them?
12. Do I make myself understood by explanations and examples?
13. Do I listen and try to understand other perspectives?
14. Do I build trust with those whom I lead?
15. Do I encourage others to participate in discussions?
16. Do I recognize the contributions of other members in the group?
17. Do I display high standards and expect the same from members?
18. Do I motivate and encourage members to follow me
19. Do I show accountability?

Nine Gifts of the Holy Spirit

1. Wisdom	2. Knowledge	3. Faith
Wisdom teaches how to apply the knowledge gained through the Holy Spirit and the ability to explain the design and nature of the gospel. It is the principal thing (Proverbs 4:7; better than gold, 16:16). It is a word spoken in season to bring comfort (Is. 50:4a).	Knowledge is supernatural revelation, which helps us to understand the mysteries of God and of spiritual things given through the Holy Spirit (II Corinthians 2:13). Knowledge distinguishes between truth and falsehood.	Without faith it is impossible to please God (Hebrews 11:6). Faith is complete trust in the sovereignty, power, and mercy of God. Faith means complete reliance upon God who is all wise, all-powerful, all knowing, and ever present.
4. Healing	**5. Miracles**	**6. Prophecy**
Performed through faith in God. Healing can be performed by the laying of hands; anointing with oil; and prayer (James 5:13-15) or by the word (Ps. 107:20; Matt. 8:8).	Miracles are divinely inspired; manifested and supernaturally. The Bible has various examples of miracles both in the Old and New Testaments.	This is divine disclosure through the Holy Spirit, for edification, exhortation and comfort of the church. Prophecy is for Believers.
7. Discernment	**8. Tongues**	**9. Interpretation of Tongues**
Being able (i). To discern the spirit world; (ii). To understand the true motives of people; (iii). To distinguish between the truth and a lie (Acts 5:3) and (v). To know the will of God.	(i). Speaking in an unknown language for praying in the spirit, worshiping and communication with God. (ii). Tongues are for a sign to the unbelievers (I Corinthians 14:22).	Translation of the message in tongues. Usually, after more than one speaker. Otherwise the speaker is advised to keep quiet and speak to himself.

Spiritual Leadership

Every Leader must assume his or her responsibilities recognizing that your faithful labour will not be in vain in the Lord.

Do not do God's work haphazardly or with constraint.

If you know you were not called by God into a certain position, politely say so, but do not accept a position to please someone else.

Similar to how God blesses a cheerful giver; He will also bless the cheerful leader in His service.

Enjoy your calling!

Suggested Reading

Buford, P.D., Griffin K., & Mangin (1986). *Spiritual Leadership & Successful Soul-winning*. Word Aflame Pentecostal Publishing House.

Beausay, W., III, (1997). *The Leadership Genius of Jesus*. Thomas Nelson Publishers.

Eims, L. (1996). *Be The Leader You Were Meant To Be*. Victor Books.

Finzel, H. (1994). *The Top Ten Mistakes Leaders Make*. Victor Books.

Greenberg, J. & Baron, R.A. (1997). *Behavior in Organizations,* (6th Ed). Prentice Hall.

Grenz, A. (1994). *The Confident Leader. Getting A Good Start As a Christian Minister*. Broadman & Holman Publishers.

Made in the USA
Charleston, SC
23 July 2010